Amphetamines

Other books in the History of Drugs series:

Amphetamines

EDITED BY NANCY HARRIS

Bruce Glassman, *Vice President*

Bonnie Szumski, *Publisher*

Helen Cothran, *Managing Editor*

GREENHAVEN PRESS

An imprint of Thomson Gale, a part of The Thomson Corporation

THOMSON

GALE

Detroit • New York • San Francisco • San Diego • New Haven, Conn.
Waterville, Maine • London • Munich

For more information, contact
Greenhaven Press
27500 Drake Rd.
Farmington Hills, MI 48331-3535
Or you can visit our Internet site at http://www.gale.com

LIBRARY OF CONGRESS CATALOGING-IN-PUBLICATION DATA

Amphetamines / Nancy Harris, book editor.
   p. cm. — (The history of drugs)
Includes bibliographical references and index.
ISBN 0-7377-1949-4 (lib. : alk. paper)
   1. Amphetamines—History—popular works. 2. Amphetamine abuse—History—Popular works. I. Harris, Nancy, 1952– . II. Series.
RM666.A493A467 2005
615'.785—dc22
                                         2004040577

CONTENTS

CHAPTER TWO: AMPHETAMINES IN THE 1980s AND 1990s

CHAPTER THREE: AMPHETAMINES TODAY

cate that recreational use of Ecstasy can lead to
serious medical problems.

Drugs are chemical compounds that affect the functioning of the body and the mind. While the U.S. Food, Drug, and Cosmetic Act defines drugs as substances intended for use in the cure, mitigation, treatment, or prevention of disease, humans have long used drugs for recreational and religious purposes as well as for healing and medicinal purposes. Depending on context, then, the term *drug* provokes various reactions. In recent years, the widespread problem of substance abuse and addiction has often given the word *drug* a negative connotation. Nevertheless, drugs have made possible a revolution in the way modern doctors treat disease. The tension arising from the myriad ways drugs can be used is what makes their history so fascinating. Positioned at the intersection of science, anthropology, religion, therapy, sociology, and cultural studies, the history of drugs offers intriguing insights on medical discovery, cultural conflict, and the bright and dark sides of human innovation and experimentation.

Drugs are commonly grouped in three broad categories: over-the-counter drugs, prescription drugs, and illegal drugs. A historical examination of drugs, however, invites students and interested readers to observe the development of these categories and to see how arbitrary and changeable they can be. A particular drug's status is often the result of social and political forces that may not necessarily reflect its medicinal effects or its potential dangers. Marijuana, for example, is currently classified as an illegal Schedule I substance by the U.S. federal government, defining it as a drug with a high potential for abuse and no currently accepted medical use. Yet in 1850 it was included in the *U.S. Pharmacopoeia* as a medicine, and solutions and tinctures containing cannabis were frequently prescribed for relieving pain and inducing sleep. In the 1930s, after smokable marijuana had gained notoriety as a recreational intoxicant, the Federal Bureau of Narcotics launched a misinformation campaign against the drug, claiming that it commonly induced insanity and murderous violence. While today's medical experts no longer make such claims about marijuana, they continue to disagree about the drug's long-term effects and medicinal potential. Most interestingly, several states have passed medical marijuana initiatives, which allow seriously ill patients compassionate access to the drug under state law—although these patients can still be prosecuted for marijuana use under federal law. Marijuana's illegal status, then, is not as fixed or final as the federal government's current schedule might suggest. Examining marijuana from a historical perspective offers readers the chance to develop a more sophisticated and critically informed view of a controversial and politically charged subject. It also encourages students to learn about aspects of medicine, history, and culture that may receive scant attention in textbooks.

Each book in Greenhaven's The History of Drugs series chronicles a particular substance or group of related drugs—discussing the appearance and earliest use of the drug in initial chapters and more recent and contemporary controversies in later chapters. With the incorporation of both primary and secondary sources written by physicians, anthropologists, psychologists, historians, social analysts, and lawmakers, each anthology provides an engaging panoramic view of its subject. Selections include a variety of readings, including book excerpts, government documents, newspaper editorials, academic articles, and personal narratives. The editors of each volume aim to include accounts of notable incidents, ideas, subcultures, or individuals connected with the drug's history as well as perspectives on the effects, benefits, dangers, and legal status of the drug.

Every volume in the series includes an introductory essay that presents a broad overview of the drug in question. The annotated table of contents and comprehensive index help readers quickly locate material of interest. Each selection is prefaced by a summary of the article that also provides any necessary historical context and biographical information on the author. Several other research aids are also present, including excerpts of supplementary material, a time line of relevant historical events, the U.S. government's current drug schedule, a fact sheet detailing drug effects, and a bibliography of helpful sources.

The Greenhaven Press The History of Drugs series gives readers a unique and informative introduction to an often-ignored facet of scientific and cultural history. The contents of each anthology provide a valuable resource for general readers as well as for students interested in medicine, political science, philosophy, and social studies.

Amphetamines were first synthetically produced in Germany in 1887. However, no medical use was found for the drug until the late 1920s. At the time medical and pharmaceutical companies, worried that supplies of ephedra, an herb used as a bronchial dilator, would be exhausted, found that amphetamines could be used as a cheap, synthetic substitute. By 1932 an amphetamine called Benzedrine was being aggressively marketed in an over-the-counter inhaler to treat nasal congestion in people with asthma, hay fever, and colds. People also used the inhalers recreationally to alter their moods, soon discovering that they could make a powerful drink by soaking the inhaler in water, coffee, or alcohol. *Consumer Reports* editor Edward M. Brecher describes a simpler method for recreational ingestion: "Users purchased Benzedrine inhalers, broke them open, and ingested the substantial quantities of amphetamines found inside."[1] Users found that Benzedrine inhalers increased wakefulness, a fact that several years later led physicians to successfully use amphetamines to treat narcolepsy, a rare sleep condition characterized by sudden attacks of deep sleep during the day. Physicians also used amphetamines to treat Parkinson's disease, an affliction characterized by tremors due to degeneration in the basal ganglia of the brain.

While testing amphetamines for medical applications in the late 1930s, researchers found that amphetamines had a positive effect on children with attention deficit hyperactivity disorder (ADHD). Although amphetamines are stimulants, the drug has the reverse effect of calming children who have trouble concentrating. Researchers also investigated amphetamines as a treatment for a variety of other health problems, including epilepsy, schizophrenia, obesity, alcoholism, opiate addiction, migraine headaches, head injuries, and radiation sickness.

Amphetamines were initially believed to have no adverse side effects. Indeed, the American Medical Association enthusiastically endorsed amphetamines, leading the general public to accept them as well. As Harvard Medical School professor Scott E. Lucas writes, "Exaggerated publicity and claims about the drugs' psychological effects contributed to the public's increased interest in amphetamine."[2] In 1937 amphetamines became available in tablet form by prescription and were prescribed liberally by physicians who believed the drugs were nonaddictive.

Amphetamines soon became available as over-the-counter "pep pills" and more people began to abuse the drug. University students used the pills to stay awake studying for exams. Truck drivers popped the pills to stay alert and avoid fatigue on long-haul drives, and truck stops along major U.S. highways became some of the earliest distribution points for amphetamines. Athletes used amphetamines to enhance performance and endurance. Businessmen, professionals, and their secretaries used amphetamines to combat fatigue and to be more productive under continuous high work pressure. Some dieters, finding that the pills decreased appetite and increased energy, took the pills for weight loss and for an energy boost.

Wartime Amphetamine Use

During World War II amphetamines were used to increase efficiency in industries and in the military forces. American, British, Japanese, and German soldiers took the pills to combat "battle fatigue." Fighter pilots, including Japanese kamikaze pilots, took amphetamines to help them stay awake and alert during long missions. Large doses of methamphetamine, a type of amphetamine, were taken by the German panzer troops to eliminate fatigue and bolster physical endurance as they rolled across Europe from 1941 to 1942. Japanese factory workers and soldiers were also large-scale consumers of methamphetamines during World War II.

Following World War II, Japan experienced a massive methamphetamine epidemic when pharmaceutical companies dumped large stocks of the drug onto the civilian market. Japan formerly had few drug problems, but in the unstable postwar environment, abuse of methamphetamines quickly spread from the slums of Japan's commercial areas to smaller towns and rural areas. In a population of approximately 89 million, 2 million persons were believed to be abusing methamphetamines during an epidemic that lasted from 1945 to 1955.

Sweden also experienced an amphetamine epidemic after World War II. Amphetamines were first introduced into Sweden in the late 1930s and were quickly restricted due to their habit-forming properties. Restrictions led to an increased underground market for amphetamines until an estimated 3 percent of the Swedish population were abusing the stimulant in the mid-1940s.

American doctors began prescribing amphetamines for depression and weight loss. An epidemic of amphetamine abuse developed in the United States following the war as well. Physicians specializing in obesity, known as "fat doctors," opened numerous clinics in the 1960s that liberally dispensed diet pills containing amphetamines. Those visiting the clinics received a brief checkup and left the clinic with a bag of pills to help them quickly lose weight. In his book, *Fat: Fighting the Obesity Epidemic*, author Robert Pool reports that "the country's fat doctors were grossing half a billion dollars a year on annual sales of two billion diet pills. Some of them were seeing as many as 100 patients a day, bringing them a total income of around $2000 daily, or half a million dollars a year."[3] Fat doctors continued their diet pill business until using amphetamines for weight loss fell out of favor because dieters suffered side effects and became addicted to the pills.

The practice of intravenous drug injection also contributed to the amphetamine epidemic in the United States in the 1960s. The practice of intravenous drug injection had been brought back to the United States by soldiers following the Korean War and had become popular on American streets. Some young Americans began using the drug to alter their moods.

They were drawn to the euphoria, enhanced motivation, and diminished need for sleep amphetamines offered.

Doctors believed that injectable amphetamines, such as the methamphetamine called Methedrine, were a safer alternative for intravenous heroin and cocaine users. Consequently, doctors began administering Methedrine to help control heroin and cocaine addiction. By the time Methedrine injections were shown to have negative effects and were withdrawn from the market, the drug had already made its way onto the streets. Methamphetamine's popularity as a street drug led to the emergence of underground meth or "speed" labs in California.

In addition to inadvertently contributing to its street use, doctors known as "Dr. Feelgoods" prescribed amphetamines to the elite, including politicians, performers, and athletes, for mood and performance enhancement. Some of these elite included former president John F. Kennedy, controversial comedian Lenny Bruce, film star Judy Garland, and the famous singers Johnny Cash and Elvis Presley.

In the sports world, speed skaters given amphetamines to increase their athleticism and stamina became ill in the 1960 Winter Olympics. Later in the Summer Olympics of the same year, Danish cyclist Knut Jensen died of an amphetamine overdose.

Consequently, several years later in 1965 laws were passed that made amphetamines in the United States illegal without a prescription. Officials passed these laws to make it harder for users to get legally manufactured amphetamines. Indeed, as the public became aware of the drug's dangers, amphetamine use decreased. The passage of the Controlled Substance Act in 1972 made amphetamines less accessible by putting further restrictions on them. However, some young people continued to use the drugs to help them stay up all night partying or studying. Studies in 1972 showed that 12 percent of youth between the ages of thirteen and twenty-five had used or were using amphetamines. Other groups such as long-haul truckers, motorcycle gangs, and athletes—including football and baseball players—continued to use amphetamines for the drug's energizing effects.

In the late 1970s and early 1980s psychiatrists quietly began administering MDMA, or Ecstasy, an amphetamine preparation. Some psychiatrists believed MDMA was effective in helping clients relax and communicate more openly and that it greatly accelerated the therapeutic process. Harvard psychiatry professor Lester Grinspoon maintained that "the general properties of MDMA warrant a full exploration of this drug as a possible catalyst to insight-oriented psychotherapy."[4] However, the Drug Enforcement Agency (DEA) became alarmed by the street use of MDMA and enforced stronger restrictions on the drug. Psychiatrists fought unsuccessfully for the right to continue using it.

Modern Amphetamine Use

Amphetamines are still used to treat narcolepsy and ADHD but doctors discourage using them for the treatment of obesity except in extreme cases. Although they are not widely used for medical purposes today, the drugs continue to be used in the military, where fighter pilots are expected to use amphetamines to remain alert on long missions. Students, athletes, and long-haul truck drivers continue to take amphetamine pills as well for their stimulating properties.

While the legal market for amphetamines has shrunk, the black market for the drugs continues to flourish. By the 1990s "ice," or crystalline methamphetamine, made its way from South Korea to Hawaii and then to mainland United States. Recreational use of "ice" and other forms of methamphetamine has swept across the continental United States. Governmental officials now consider the recreational use of methamphetamines to be epidemic. DEA administrator Donnie R. Marshall stated that "it is fair to say that methamphetamine is one of the most significant law enforcement and social issues facing our nation today, and it has affected specific regions of the country in a dramatic fashion."[5] Methamphetamine use is increasing in the workplace where people use the drug to do a better job, alleviate fatigue, and enable them to work overtime. Others use methamphetamines to lose weight, to increase confidence, to boost energy, or to appear more cheerful. Although amphetamines were originally synthesized for medical purposes, they are used vastly more as a recreational drug today.

Notes

1. Edward M. Brecher, *Licit and Illicit Drugs*. Boston: Little, Brown, 1972, p. 278.

2. Scott E. Lucas, *Amphetamines*. New York: Chelsea House, 1985, p. 20.

3. Robert Pool, *Fat: Fighting the Obesity Epidemic*. New York: Oxford University Press, 2001, p. 199.

4. Quoted in Kathryn Rose Gertz, "Hug Drug," *Harper's Bazaar*, vol. 119, November 1985, p. 48.

5. Donnie R. Marshall, congressional testimony given before the Senate Judiciary Committee, July 28, 1999.

CHAPTER ONE

Early Amphetamines

A Historical Overview of Amphetamines

Lester Grinspoon and Peter Hedblom

In this selection, Lester Grinspoon and Peter Hedblom trace the history of amphetamines from their first synthesis in 1887 through the 1960s, when "speed freaks" abused the drug. Drug companies first made amphetamines available to the public with the marketing of Benzedrine, an over-the-counter inhalant for nasal congestion. Chemists and drug companies soon developed a prosperous market, free from safety restrictions. The availability and overprescription of the drugs led to widespread abuse and the eventual outlawing of amphetamine inhalers. However, amphetamines were still legal in tablet form. During World War II, abuse of the drug grew worse when millions of amphetamines were dispensed to soldiers on both sides of the war. The military became a virtual breeding ground for the illegal use of amphetamines. Long-haul truckers in the United States also contributed to amphetamine abuse. By the 1960s, experts estimated that 4 billion tablets, half the legal production, had been illegally consumed. At this time, intravenous users, known as speed freaks, were starting to manufacture amphetamines in home labs. Lester Grinspoon is a practicing psychiatrist and associate professor of psychiatry at Harvard Medical School. He has authored twelve books, including, *Marihuana Reconsidered*. Peter Hedblom coauthored *The American Speed-Culture: Amphetamines in the U.S. Today* with Lester Grinspoon.

Lester Grinspoon and Peter Hedblom, "Amphetamines Reconsidered," *Saturday Review of Science*, vol. 55, July 8, 1972, pp. 33–46. Copyright © 1972 by General Media International, Inc. Reproduced by permission of the publisher.

Historically, there is ample evidence that drug abuse antedated drug therapy, just as toxicology paved the way for pharmacology. Primitive man seems to have been more interested in poisons than in medicines. Even the Greek physician Hippocrates, although he recommended natural salicylates from willow trees for eye disease and the pain associated with childbirth, considered most drugs essentially useless. (However, when the Athenians decided to dispose of Socrates, they had a most effective herb on hand.) Today [1972], in the case of amphetamines, the tape is being run backward at increasing speed. Pharmacology is reverting to toxicology. Abuse of these truly addicting and dangerous drugs has reached frightening proportions. For example, of the more than twelve billion standard-dose amphetamine tablets produced in 1971, an estimated 50 per cent were diverted to the flourishing black market to supplement huge amounts of "home-cooked speed."

In 1887 the German pharmacologist L. Edeleano first synthesized phenylisopropylamine, the drug that would eventually become famous as Benzedrine. However, he was not interested in exploring its pharmacological properties and put this extraordinary stimulant at the back of the shelf. Not until 1910 did G. Barger and Sir H.H. Dale investigate the effects on experimental animals of this and a series of closely related chemical compounds that they called "sympathomimetic amines." [Sympathomimetic refers to having an effect similar to that produced when the sympathetic nervous system is stimulated.] But no one in America or England grasped the implications of their findings for another seventeen years. Although Barger and Dale did hint that some of these drugs might possess powerful central nervous system–stimulating properties, the only point that seemed of interest to the few readers who digested their technical and dense paper was that most of these sympathomimetic amines had essentially the same alerting effects on the physiological systems of cats (and presumably humans) as did epinephrine (adrenaline), the first hormone to be synthesized.

Search for an Ephedrine Substitute

The next pharmacological advance toward the eventual redis-
covery of the amphetamines was initiated by the Chinese
physician-pharmacologist K.K. Chen, who embarked on a
comprehensive analysis of the ancient codifications of naturally occurring (herbal) drugs. Chen was struck by the large
number of references, beginning in 2760 B.C., to the desert
herb *Ma Huang* (*Ephedra vulgaris*) as a specific remedy for
asthma and other respiratory ailments. Chen learned that the
active principle of *Ma Huang* was the alkaloid ephedrine, which
was very closely related to epinephrine. Accordingly, Chen and
his colleague, C.F. Schmidt, in 1924 published the results of
their preliminary investigations, pointing out that ephedrine
was superior to epinephrine. As a direct result of this and sub-
sequent reporting by Chen and Schmidt, the medical use of
ephedrine increased at such a fantastic rate that some physicians began to fear that natural supplies would be exhausted.
Consequently, research pharmacologists set out on a new
search for an ephedrine substitute. [Doctor of internal medicine and allergies] George Piness was aware of Edeleano's discovery and suggested to [British chemist] Gordon Alles, who
was engaged in research involving amino acids, that Alles
might shift his energies to looking for a synthetic amine substitute for ephedrine. Alles in 1927 confirmed Piness's hunch
by concluding that the most effective such substitute was the
original amphetamine synthesized by Edeleano. It was Alles
who first named this drug Benzedrine, because, when it was
exposed to air, it rapidly changed to the carbonate that has the
chemical name *benzyl-methyl-carbinamine*.

Because of his willingness to use himself as a human
guinea pig, Alles quickly discovered that amphetamine was
active whether inhaled or taken orally, and he also found that
Benzedrine was surpassed by its dextro (right-handed) isomer
in its ability to alleviate fatigue, increase or intensify his alert-
ness, and make him feel euphorically confident, even when it

kept him awake long into the night. This dextro isomer was eventually marketed as dextro-amphetamine, or Dexedrine.

First Commercial Application of Amphetamine

F.P. Nabenhauer, the chief chemist at the drug house of Smith, Kline & French, soon found out about Alles's work and began to experiment with various commercial applications of amphetamine in conjunction with his firm's patented inhaling device. The executives at Smith, Kline & French realized the potential bonanza this new class of synthetic ephedrine substitute represented and persuaded Alles to sell them all his patent rights. In 1932 their Benzedrine inhaler was first made available to the public, by nonprescription, over-the-counter sale in drugstores across the country. The American Medical Association [AMA] gave this new drug the generic name "amphetamine," from *alpha-methyl-phenethyl-amine*. In a mild parenthetical warning note, the AMA cautioned that "continued overdosage" might cause "restlessness and sleeplessness," but it also assured physicians that "no serious reactions have been observed." In late 1937 the AMA approved the new drug in tablet form, recognizing it as an acceptable therapeutic medication for the treatment of narcolepsy and also of postencephalitic Parkinsonism. The AMA further stated that Benzedrine was "useful" in the treatment of "certain depressive psychopathic conditions" and that persons "under the strict supervision of a physician" could even take amphetamine in order to capture "a sense of increased energy or capacity for work, or a feeling of exhilaration."

Amphetamines Gain Popularity

Soon the nation's several media (especially *Time* magazine, which called the new drug "poisonous") were giving amphetamines a considerable amount of sensational publicity, all of which did nothing to discourage use. Quite to the contrary, the numerous references to these "brain," "pep," and "superman" pills in the popular press, even when phrased ostensibly as warnings, acted mainly to arouse the curiosity and interest of the American people. Most important, however, was the quick and amazingly enthusiastic reception accorded these inhalers and pills by the medical profession. The AMA was especially influential in reinforcing the general impression that this was indeed a new wonder drug.

Public attitudes toward the amphetamines initially (and for many years) were either positive, neutral, or merely humorous. The persons who used them did not, in the vast majority of cases, fit into any traditional stereotypes of "dope fiends." As long as the medical community was willing to accept the manufacturers' claims, no one was going to question why, in 1932, virtually any new psychoactive "medicine" could be marketed without any proof of either safety or efficacy. Nor did the AMA, the Food and Drug Administration, or the Federal Bureau of Narcotics have any legal or sublegal authority to deny a drug company the right to sell nearly any chemical not specifically forbidden by the Harrison Act of 1914. For example, all the Food and Drug Administration could do was to recommend appropriate therapeutic indications; it had absolutely no power to limit or warn against consumer purchasing of drugs for which prescriptions were not required, and the last nonprescription amphetamine inhaler was not removed from the market until 1971. Furthermore, the amphetamines clearly demonstrated the ease with which drug manufacturers could expand claims for their products and advertise their usefulness in an unlimited range of areas. Some drug firms obtained patents for their amphetamine congeners and combinations on the basis of these drugs' alleged "antidepressant" actions and then expanded their advertising claims to include the "treatment" of conditions as disparate as obesity, alcoholism, enuresis [bed-wetting] and so on. Other firms followed different paths, starting from the claim that their product was "uniquely effective" in the treatment of obesity but employing the same basic tactics. Somehow, supporting articles and thinly disguised testimonials invariably appeared in "reputable" medical organs, such as the *Journal of the American Medical Association*, just prior to the publication of advertisements extending the reasons for prescribing amphetamines. Although only a few of these reports were exposed as fraudulent, most of them were clearly biased, did not use random sampling or double-blind techniques, and frequently drew dubious conclusions. Complementing the enthusiastic overprescribing of amphetamines by physicians is the fact that since the 1930s there have been other ways in which the public could procure these "euphoriants." In short, amphetamines can be secured with little or no assistance by or interference from organized medicine, the Food and Drug Administration, or any state or federal drug abuse control authorities.

Inhalers Are Abused

First, there were the inhalers. Although Smith, Kline & French held the patent on the Benzedrine inhaler until 1950, other drug companies quickly realized that they could sell their own imitations without fear of patent-infringement suit because Benzedrine was only one of an almost unlimited variety of equally stimulating, euphorigenic, and toxic amphetamine congeners. By the end of World War II there were at least seven different inhalers containing large amounts of these drugs on the market, and all of them could be purchased without a prescription at drug or grocery stores. All were easy to break open, and the number of techniques of ingestion was limited only by the ingenuity of the abusers. Although soaking the cotton fillers in alcohol or in coffee and then drinking the solution produced the desired effects, a much stronger kick could be obtained by chewing on these bits of cotton or by simply swallowing them whole. The extent of inhaler abuse was finally documented in the medical literature by the now classic study conducted by R.R. Monroe and H.H. Drell in late 1947. They found that about 25 per cent of more than 1,000 military prisoners questioned openly admitted to abuse of amphetamine inhalers. Monroe and Drell stressed that their figures were "deceptively low" because amphetamine intoxication was considered a grave offense by the military prison authorities. The actual extent of inhaler abuse may have exceeded 40 per cent in this army-stockade population. Prison life could not be blamed; more than 95 per cent of the men had begun to take amphetamines after induction into the army but before incarceration. It was apparent that these men resorted to inhalers because, unlike soldiers outside stockades, they did not have access to Benzedrine in pill form. Monroe and Drell were also careful to point out that most of these prisoners were not criminals but "essentially normal persons who were merely victims of circumstances or severe situational stress."

Inhalers Are Banned

In the years following issuance of the Monroe report the abuse of amphetamine inhalers became such an obvious sociomedical problem that many drug firms withdrew their products from the market. The remaining drug firms were supposedly forced to drop their inhalers in 1959, when these amphetamine sources were finally banned by the Food and Drug Administration except as prescription items. However, this ban was almost totally ineffective as it applied only to devices containing Benzedrine and dextro-amphetamine. This left a major loophole that was seized upon by a number of drug houses. In fact, one small Midwest firm began to market its Valo inhaler containing 150 mg of methamphetamine, *after* the Food and Drug Administration ban had gone into effect. The ultimate in inhaler abuse—intravenous injection of the contents—was first reported in 1959 and was soon fairly widespread. As late as March of 1970 [psychiatrist Burton] M. Angrist and his co-workers reported four cases of amphetamine psychosis resulting from abuse of the Wyamine inhaler, which contained 250 mg of mephenter-mine [less stimulating amphetamine-type agent] representing ten to twenty times the usually prescribed central nervous system–stimulating dose. The Wyamine inhaler was finally withdrawn from the market on June 22, 1971, because of pressure from the Justice Department. But, even though inhalers introduced millions of young people to amphetamines, most users found that it was just as easy to procure the pills. In the first three years after Benzedrine was introduced in tablet form, sales climbed to more than fifty million units.

World War II Spurs Abuse

World War II probably was responsible for spurring both the legal medically authorized use and the illegal black-market abuse of the amphetamines. When German Panzer troops overwhelmed Poland, then Denmark and Norway, and drove through Belgium and France, they were taking huge doses of methamphetamine to eliminate fatigue and maintain physical endurance. But the Wehrmacht [German army] was by no means the sole large-scale consumer of amphetamines during World War II; Japanese soldiers and factory workers used as much or more. Nor was use of these stimulants confined to the Axis powers. According to British war statistics, seventy-two million standard-dose amphetamine tablets were distributed to the British armed forces alone. Although the U.S. armed forces did not authorize the issuing of amphetamines on a regular basis until the time of the Korean conflict, Benzedrine was used extensively by army air corps personnel stationed in Britain, and it was an open secret that many pilots were engaged in a mammoth bootlegging operation. Amphetamines were also easily obtainable from military medical officers and aides. The amount of Benzedrine supplied to U.S. servicemen by the British has been estimated at nearly 80 million tablets and pills, and probably another 80 to 100 million were supplied by U.S. Army medics.

If only 10 per cent of the American fighting men ever used amphetamines during World War II, more than 1.5 million returned to this country with some firsthand knowledge of the effects of these drugs. Indeed, in recent years the armed forces have constituted a veritable breeding ground for the abuse of all kinds of drugs, especially the amphetamines. . . .

Amphetamines as Versatile Remedies

By 1946 Smith, Kline & French had been so successful in its amphetamine promotion campaign that a paper by [British physician] W.R. Bett listed thirty-nine generally accepted "clinical uses" for the drug including treatments of schizophrenia, morphine and codeine addictions, nicotinism (tobacco smoking), heart block, head injuries, infantile cerebral palsy, irradiation sickness, and hypotension (abnormally low blood pressure). Bett, who further recommended the drug for such ailments as sea sickness, persistent hiccups, and even "caffeine mania," was only one of a huge number of physicians who regarded amphetamines as "versatile remedies" that were second only to a few other extraordinary drugs (such as aspirin) in terms of the scope, efficacy and safety of their effects.

Today [in 1972] even though the Food and Drug Administration officially recognizes only "short-term appetite reduction," narcolepsy, some types of Parkinsonism, and certain behavioral disorders in so-called hyperkinetic young children as valid "therapeutic indications" for the amphetamines this federal agency lacks real power to limit the drug industry's advertising claims. Amphetamines continue to be prescribed by many physicians for nearly as many different reasons as Bett mentioned. . . .

Truckers Contribute to Black-Market Speed

Many published studies continue to report amphetamine use rates that are gross underestimates because they ignore the incredibly widespread black-market distribution system that continues to thrive despite federal efforts to seal up the massive leakage from pharmaceutical companies, wholesalers, druggists, and even physicians' offices. What has become a multimillion-dollar, organized crime–controlled business began in all-night restaurants and gasoline stations that catered to long-haul truck drivers, one of the first groups to discover the fatigue-alleviating and sleep-postponing properties of the amphetamines.

(Some of the early slang names for amphetamines originated among these truck drivers, who called them "cartwheels," "coast-to-coasts," "West-Coast turnarounds," "truck drivers," and "copilots." The last term presumably was derived from the now legendary accident that occurred when one exceedingly lucky driver, who had stayed behind his wheel for more than two days on speed, decided to take a brief nap in his sleeping berth while moving at 60 miles per hour. When finally extricated from his totally demolished vehicle, he stated that he had been sure that his assistant was competent to handle the truck in broad daylight. The "copilot," however, was an amphetamine-induced illusion; the driver had been alone for the entire forty-eight-hour period.)

The built-in "mobility" of this early illicit amphetamine distribution system was probably one of the main reasons for the extraordinary rapidity of its spread to all sections of the country. . . .

Controls Are Too Few and Ineffectual

In January 1965 Representative Olen Harris introduced the Drug Abuse Control Amendments of 1965. Despite predictable opposition from the American health industry, this bill was finally passed by Congress. The law, seeking to impose greater controls, required increased record keeping throughout all parts of the system of manufacture, distribution, prescription, and sale. The punishments for violations were not severe; the maximum penalties were two years in prison and/or a $5,000 fine. In fact, the Drug Abuse Control Amendents of 1965 were a prime example of too few of the wrong controls too late. Nothing was done about reducing drug industry profits or controlling the overproduction of amphetamines by setting sensible quotas or empowering the Food and Drug Administration to do more than "advise" what the "acceptable therapeutic applications" should be. The controls that were instituted proved to be dismally unenforceable and totally ineffectual in short-circuiting the continued flow of pharmaceutical amphetamines to the black market. Underground entrepreneurs simply refined their techniques. For example, the syndicate-controlled illegal amphetamine marketers discovered that it was easy to transfer amphetamines from the legitimate distribution system by having them shipped to drug houses and "repackagers" in Mexico and then smuggled or mailed back across the border. This strategy was based on a loophole in the 1965–66 legislation that totally exempted amphetamines if they were to be shipped abroad. According to the 1971 *Fourth Report* of the Select Committee on Crime, U.S. Customs had reported a 212 per cent increase in *seizures* of contraband amphetamines during the previous two years. But this statistic gives only some suggestion as to the enormous volume of U.S.-produced amphetamines that enter the black market by this circuitous crossing and recrossing of international borders. For example, on January 19, 1972, *The New York Times* reported that Strasenburgh Prescription Products had shipped almost a ton of bulk amphetamine to Strasenburgh's Mexican affiliate, where it was packaged in 25-mg Bifetamina capsules and sold to Mexican *farmacias* near the Texas border. Many of these "retail drugstores" were shacks, out in empty fields far from any towns, where smugglers picked up huge quantities of "black beauties" to carry back to the United States. According to a spokesman for the Narcotics Bureau, the number of these Strasenburgh capsules smuggled into the United States probably approached forty-five million per year. At the present time the one decisive difference between the organized black markets in amphetamines and in heroin derives from the fact that the diversion of amphetamines is conducted so efficiently and skillfully, and on so huge a scale, that the illicit price which the addict or abuser pays on the street is just about exactly the same as he would pay for his drugs if he obtained them through strictly legal channels. This, of course, is in sharp contrast to the business in heroin.

Home-Cooked Speed Suppliers

Legitimate drug producers, however are not the only black-market suppliers. In fact, in some sections of this country the manufacture and sale of "home-cooked" speed is thought to exceed the legal pharmaceutical production by a factor of between three and ten. This illicit manufacture is a fairly recent development in the history of amphetamines. The spiraling criminal traffic in black-market speed resulted in a 1963 request from the California attorney general's office that the commercial manufacturers of injectable amphetamines discontinue their sale of these ampules. The manufacturers complied, but almost immediately the first clandestine laboratory for mass production of injectable amphetamines was set up in San Francisco. By 1968 there were between five and ten of these labs within the Bay Area, each supplying the San Francisco speed scene with about 25 to 100 pounds of illegally produced amphetamines per week. An unknown number of smaller "bathroom" laboratories, located mostly in Haight-Ashbury [a neighborhood in San Francisco], were contributing again as much speed, and numerous formulas describing the synthesis of the final products were being hawked on every street in the Haight.

The Japanese Methamphetamine Epidemic of the Post–World War II Era

Henry Brill and Tetsuya Hirose

The following selection is a report from the National Institute on Drug Abuse describing the abuse of methamphetamine in Japan after World War II. Methamphetamine, a type of amphetamine, first appeared in Japan in 1940 and was used for the treatment of mental disorders, narcolepsy (a sleep disorder), and weight reduction. After World War II the large stocks of the drug that previously had been produced for military consumption were no longer needed. Pharmaceutical companies released these drugs onto the market, contributing to widespread abuse. Interestingly, three times as many females used the methamphetamines as males. At the height of the epidemic of methamphetamine abuse in 1954, an estimated 2 milllion people were using the drug. Although the Japanese brought the abuse under control in 1955 through strict legislation and enforcement practices, other illegal drugs such as heroin became prevalent on the streets. The National Institute on Drug Abuse is part of the National Institutes of Health, a division of the U.S. Department of Health and Human Services. It conducts research on the effects of drug abuse and addiction.

Henry Brill is a psychiatrist and director of Pilgrim State Psychiatric Hospital in New York City. He is also editor of *Ge-*

Henry Brill and Tetsuya Hirose, "The Rise and Fall of a Methamphetamine Epidemic: Japan, 1945–1955," *Seminars in Psychiatry*, vol. 1, 1969, pp. 179–94. Copyright © 1969 by the National Institute on Drug Abuse. Reproduced by permission.

netic Research in Psychiatry. Tetsuya Hirose is a professor of psychiatry at Teikyo University's School of Medicine in Japan.

From 1945 to 1955 Japan experienced a wave of abuse of methamphetamine. This outbreak, which is unique in many respects, constitutes one of the most important chapters in the history of drug dependence. It arose in a population that had been singularly free of all types of drug dependence; furthermore, methamphetamine itself was a relatively new drug, having been introduced into Japanese medicine as recently as 1940. In this outbreak of drug abuse the agent was well defined, the date of onset known, and the sequence of events clearly delineated. The pattern of spread and the nature of the involved population were well documented, as were the nature and prevalence of various types of adverse reactions. Finally, the termination of the episode was fully recorded. . . .

There had never been a problem of drug dependence of any kind in Japan and only towards the end of the epidemic did other drugs of dependence begin to play any significant role. The epidemic followed a clear course of spectacular increase with a sharp peak and a rapid decline after 1945–1955.

The first cases were noted in 1945 in the slums of major commercial and industrial centers of Japan. From there the drug spread to smaller towns and thence to the rural areas. Shortly, no prefecture of all Japan was free of methamphetamine addicts. The problem was clearly caused by the release of large stocks of methamphetamine, among other war surplus items, by pharmaceutical houses and other sources of supply. The drug was largely in ampule form and the route of administration described was almost universally parenteral [injected]. The problems of methamphetamine abuse became so pervasive that in July 1948 methamphetamine was listed as a dangerous drug and a law was passed to control "awakening drugs" more effectively. At this time, a "home brew" variety began to appear. As law enforcement became more effective, the methamphetamine content of the ampules decreased. In June of 1951, a second Awakening Drug (Wake-amine) Control law was passed and in 1953 a massive public education campaign was initiated. The law was further strengthened in 1954 and 1955.

The peak of the epidemic appears to have been reached in 1954. The decline of the outbreak was strikingly rapid and by 1957 there were relatively few cases. Since then the problem has been a minor one. However, as amphetamine abuse declined, there was a sharp rise in heroin addiction followed by a series of other drug dependence problems.

Japanese Methamphetamine Abusers

The first cases were predominantly writers, musicians and artists. However, within a short time a strong affinity for economically marginal and delinquent groups became clearly manifest. The Korean minority were particularly involved apparently because of their position of social and economic disadvantage. The Chinese, too, were disproportionately involved.

The disorder was primarily one of young males. Those arrested were usually between 12 and 25 years old and the age of onset of drug use lay between 16 and 20. They had a history of disturbed life patterns which could be traced back as far as the age of 10 and delinquent behavior often preceded drug use.

The psychiatric syndromes resulting from methamphetamine abuse observed in Japan differ from those described in other countries; Western literature tends to report a higher proportion of schizophrenic-like reactions. In Japan, however, a wider dispersion of syndromes was found with one large study showing 8% of the addicts tended to be diagnosed as psychopathic, 23% manic-depressive, 19% mixed manic and schizophrenic and 31% apathetic exhausted states.

In Japan the proportion of female to male drug offenders was far higher (3:1) than the proportion of female to male drug offenders generally. These female drug addicts tended also to be more recalcitrant, aggressive and difficult to manage in correctional facilities than the males. Mental defects played no role in drug dependence and non-addicted delinquents showed more than twice as much mental retardation as the addicted. One investigator reviewed the problem of the relation between psychoses and the taking of methamphetamine and concluded that the addict is a disturbed, weak individual before his addiction and this leads him into abuse of drugs but the drugs aggravate the basic problem and create new ones.

The age distribution curve of the methamphetamine group admitted to mental hospitals differed from the schizophrenic group in having a sharp peak at the age group 20–25. Also, they had much less family history of schizophrenia. While there was a preponderance of socially deprived among the drug takers there was considerable representation from other classes of persons and it was clear that the epidemic was by no means limited to any class.

The average dose of methamphetamine injected by abusers was 90 mg of methamphetamine per day taken for more than 3 months. However, daily doses varied across a range of up to 1,200 mg per day. Despite the vast amount of intravenous drug use there appears to be no mention of hepatitis.

Japanese methamphetamine abusers were not basically different from those described in the Western literature as to age, sex, distribution, socioeconomic class, tendency to delinquency and to social disability. There was some tendency to see a proportion of manic-depressive patterns in the personalities of these addicts. In contrast, Western literature emphasizes the preponderance of a paranoid schizophrenic syndrome.

Methamphetamine: The Agent

There is a tendency to refer to the amphetamines generally as the primary Japanese problem but evidence suggests that only methamphetamine was involved. Methamphetamine was known in Japan as "Philopon" and by other names. The epidemic is attributed by all authors to the release of stocks of methamphetamine at the close of hostilities. The drug itself had first appeared in Japan in 1940, at which time it was recommended for the treatment of mental disorder, narcolepsy and weight reduction.

The Japanese did not consider methamphetamine a hazard in 1945 when the stores were released. In accordance with the prevailing regulations of that country, the drug was available without prescription.

Environmental Factors Promote Drug Dependence

It is difficult to think of an environmental situation more conducive to an explosive outbreak of drug dependence than that which developed in Japan immediately after the close of World War II. At this time, Japan was plunged into a series of vast and cataclysmic social changes.

Following the war, the long-term trend toward massive urbanization was resumed. By 1965 the population of the country exceeded 98 million of which some 53 million were living in urban centers. To the stress of these vast population movements were added a radical democratization of the government and a loosening of the traditional authority structure of the country. It was a time of military occupation, complicated by major changes of economic, social, educational, administrative and even the moral aspects of Japanese life. Decentralization, demilitarization, land reform and moves to break up large estates and large industrial organizations was in progress. A radical new constitution had been adopted and the country was shaken by a series of labor disturbances involving unprecedented threats of a general strike. It was at this time that large supplies of methamphetamine were released for purchase over the counter. . . .

When we recall the massive Japanese experience of the early 1950s and when we note that by 1953 and 1954 Japan was engaged in an all out struggle to control a tidal wave of methamphetamine abuse, it is almost incredible that still in 1958 and afterwards there could have been serious debate in Britain, Sweden and the United States as to the potential hazards of substances of this type. However, the Japanese experience has now been duplicated in the West, although on a far smaller scale.

The 1946–1954 epidemic of intravenous methamphetamine abuse in Japan anticipated the course of events in other countries by more than a full decade. It provided a clear demonstration of the nature and characteristics of such an epidemic, identified the vulnerable population and described the psychiatric and behavior disorders to be expected.

The "Splash" Scene of the Early 1960s in the United States

John William Rawlin

"Splash," referring to intravenously injected amphetamines, got its name from the feeling it gave users of having ice-cold water thrown into their face. Splash was introduced on the street in the late 1950s when heroin became less available and more likely to be of poor quality. Although some heroin users did not like splash because of its side effects, including hair loss and heart trouble, young splashers liked amphetamines because the drug helped them to be more sociable and alert. In the early 1960s, operators of "splash houses" held parties and made huge profits by selling amphetamine powder doctored with ingredients such as powdered milk, Epsom salts, and baking soda. Some splashers supported their habit through petty theft or by breaking into cars. Police generally found splash addicts more violent than heroin addicts. In this selection, John William Rawlin describes a midwestern metropolitan area where the amphetamine subculture flourished. At the time of publication, Rawlin served on the faculty of the sociology department of Southern Illinois University.

Splash came to the [midwestern metropolitan area observed in this study] in the late 1950's. (Splash is a local term referring to amphetamine hydrochloride sulphate when shot intravenously by the user.) The introduction of amphetamines on the street came at a time when the heroin market was precarious. Pressure was on because of the wounding of a Federal investigator, who, nevertheless, had broken the ring of pushers. The local crime syndicate had decided to get out of the amphetamine market, leaving the field open to independent operators, or "cowboys" who in turn were being arrested quite regularly. Heroin was not only scarce, but of increasingly poor quality, most of it 3 per cent pure or less. Splash filled the void, slowly at first, but rapidly increasing until in 1963 it was the chief drug in use on the streets.

As the use of amphetamines spread locally, slang was developed to describe it. Most of the words are common elsewhere, but the meanings vary somewhat with locale. "Splash" was used in both a generic sense, that is to refer to all the amphetamines, powders or ampules, and sometimes in a specific sense to refer to amphetamine sulphate. Splash was so named, it is said, because the effect of shooting it is like having "ice cold water thrown in your face." It is claimed by many to cause penile erections and sometimes orgasm.

"Spliven," "grease" and "rhythm" are other names used interchangeably for the amphetamines. Spliven is sometimes used to refer to methyl amphetamine hydrochloride, or to dextro amphetamine sulphate and is preferred over splash by some abusers who claim that you hallucinate less on spliven and it gives you more drive. Several abusers explain the difference between spliven and splash as being like the difference betwen whisky and wine.

Use of amphetamine in pill or capsule form is graded as the lowest level of usage by the abusers. This is followed by "vaylo usage" [a slang term referring to a middle level of usage]; and then on the highest level of usage is splash and spliven. A few of the older heroin users were opposed to splash except as a temporary measure, and the switch from heroin was by no means a complete conversion. The conflict over splash pitted these older heroin users against the younger majority who were pro-splash. The old users argued that splash is weaker than heroin and should be used only in emergency or in combination with heroin. The physical consequences of using amphetamines worried them: "your hair falls out," "it's bad for your heart," or "it makes you crazy." Suspicious of the unpredictable behavior of the splash user, they believed that it interfered with hustling activities and brought heat on the system.

Younger Amphetamine Users

Aligned for splash were the younger users who had switched from heroin or who had always used amphetamines. While they admitted that heroin might have been more powerful in the past, it was no longer true. Referring to the way heroin was sometimes cut, a young user taunted an older user, "You ain't shooting nothing but scouring powder, man, you are the Bon Ami Kid." [Bon Ami is a brand of scouring powder.] In a group discussion on the power of the two drugs, one user of splash who had previously used heroin for eight years argued that both drugs were probably equally potent but in different ways; and pointed out that the two drugs did different things for you and could not be compared on the dimension of potency. Many of the younger users chose the stimulating effects of amphetamines over the dreamy, somnolent effects of the narcotics on much the same basis that they liked rock and roll music and rejected the blues. Splash suited the contemporary mood—it encouraged you to talk, dance and be sociable. The advocates for amphetamines were not convinced that it made them less efficient at hustling—they pointed out that splash made them more alert and gave them "more heart." While tripping (the hallucinations that sometimes result from use of splash) admittedly made the user vulnerable, his situation was no worse than that of the anxious heroin user. And his habit could be controlled by barbiturates. Furthermore, the pro-amphetamine majority argued, supplies were easier to get and were available from more sources. Despite the conflict, intravenous use of amphetamines came to be accepted as more than a substitute during periods when heroin was unavailable, and became the drug of first choice for a majority of the drug users in the area.

Obtaining Splash

The user could obtain splash in several ways. He could legitimately obtain it by prescription, or by stealing prescription blanks and forging them. A few drugstores would supply amphetamines without a prescription. Most likely, however, he purchased the drug from a pusher at prices ranging from $1.00 to $2.00 a cap. It was sometimes sold by papers or "bindles." The other popular method was to obtain it at a splash house or a splash party.

Originally the splash parties were simply informal gatherings that grew out of the amphetamine user's sociable inclination to indulge his habit in the company of his fellows. Eventually these parties became more organized and evolved into the splash house, an extremely lucrative operation. The operators of splash houses are usually able to get amphetamine powder at about $9.00 an ounce, which they then adulterate with such cheap extenders as powdered milk, epsom salts, baking soda, quinine and powdered sugar. By such means one woman who operated a splash house in the area was able to make the remarkable profit of $3,000.00 from a $9.00 investment in amphetamine powder.

Pushers obtained supplies of splash by three main methods. During the early period, robbing pharmaceutical supply warehouses in the area provided a substantial amount of splash, but this source disappeared in 1963 when the pharmaceutical companies stopped storing amphetamine in the area. A few drugstores ordered large quantities of various amphetamines for sale to users and pushers. Amphetamines could be ordered from smaller pharmaceutical outlets under the pretense of scientific research. Few amphetamines manufactured by major companies were seen on the street. However, "vaylo" inhalers were not uncommon before they were restricted to prescription use, and some use of the 35¢ Vicks inhaler was made by some younger, beginning users.

Using Amphetamines

The novice can start shooting amphetamines intravenously, but usually it is the practice to start by pill-popping or by the sub-lingual method. Sometimes the amphetamine is used in combi-nation with another drug or food, for example, "vaylo" strips are ingested by dipping them in liquids or sometimes eaten on bread as a sandwich. Some users warn against eating cheese while using amphetamines. Apparently this has some merit.

The regular user adopts the intravenous method, using an eye dropper or a No. 26 hypodermic needle, but preferring a Murine eye dropper because it is usually cleaner. The peculiar sharing habits of amphetamine users make them susceptible to infection from dirty needles. One instance is known of forty cases of hepatitis resulting from one dirty needle. There are several techniques for injection with the eye dropper, one aim-ing at the quickest and fastest way of forcing the powder into the vein, and the other at a more prolonged reaction. The de-tails of either technique is apt to shock the sensibilities of even the moderately squeamish. There is less concern among the amphetamine abusers than among heroin users for the ritual of taking the drug, but in contrast to the older heroin user, the younger splashers talk about and anticipate the effects of the drug—what it will do for you.

The hustle of the splasher is much the same as that of the "snatch and grab" junkie. That is, they support their habits through petty theft or breaking into cars. A majority of the girls are prostitutes, but few of the males are fortunate enough to have girls who are willing to prostitute or shoplift for them.

The relation of drug use to violent crime is a hard question to answer. For the heroin user, crimes of violence are not as common as crimes against property, and many of the reports of violent behavior resulting from amphetamine use have come from the users themselves. They have described hallucinations with persecution themes that resulted in attacks on innocent bystanders, friends, or policemen, and some abusers report that violent "stompings" by teen-agers have resulted from splashing.

While some claim that splash makes them sexually potent, there have been no reports of sexual assaults by users in the area. Although one prostitute was found strangled, her assailant was not a drug user. Verbal violence in the form of "joining" (a local term for "playing the dozens" [exchanging insults]) was common in groups of amphetamine abusers, but could not be considered distinctive, since it is also quite common to the youth of the larger Negro community. Police reports claim that because of his violent behavior the splasher is much harder to arrest than the relatively cool heroin junkie, and there is no doubt that use of splash evokes violent behavior in some. There is no evidence that this violent behavior is translated into violent crimes.

A Controversial Doctor Prescribes Amphetamines to the Elite in the 1960s

Time

This 1972 selection from *Time* magazine calls into question the practice of Max Jacobson, a German-born physician who reportedly routinely gave amphetamine injections to his patients throughout the 1960s. These patients included dozens of leading writers, politicians, and jet-setters who were given the powerful stimulants to lift their moods and help their performances. They had mixed reactions to the amphetamine treatments: Some said the injections enhanced their careers, while others claimed to suffer terribly from the treatments. At least one patient died of an overdose. Jacobson defended his practice of dispensing amphetamines. The American Medical Association, however, regarded amphetamine abuse as widespread and asked all doctors to limit the drug's use to only those conditions for which it was specifically indicated.

Dr. Max Jacobson accompanied President John F. Kennedy to his 1961 summit meeting with [the president of the Soviet Union] Nikita Khrushchev in Vienna, visited Kennedy at the White House and was often heard to boast that he treated both the Chief Executive and his wife. . . . The New York *Times* reported that the German-born general practitioner could have done a good deal more name-dropping from his roster of rich and famous patients. The *Times* also suggested that those patients were getting some startling treatments. Dr. Jacobson, said the *Times*, had been dispensing amphetamines, the powerful stimulants known to the drug culture as "speed." He had given injections to dozens of the country's leading writers, politicians and jet-setters to elevate their moods and help them to perform better.

The story takes pains to point out that there is no proof that either President or Mrs. Kennedy received amphetamines from Jacobson. Nor does it say which of those on Jacobson's patient list—which included such names as Author Truman Capote, Playwright Tennessee Williams, Singer Eddie Fisher and the late President's [John F. Kennedy] brother-in-law, Prince Stanislas Radziwill—actually got speed. But the story does establish that amphetamines were often a part of Jacobson's prescriptions.

Many of Jacobson's patients regard him as a virtual magician whose treatments have been essential to their careers. Others have found the price of performance too high. Amphetamine users often become heavily dependent on the drug, which can produce the symptoms of schizophrenia. Many amphetamine users experience delusions and feelings of paranoia; some become depressed and suicidal.

Several of Jacobson's patients suffered bad effects from their treatment. Film Producer Otto Preminger, a patient for a short time, quit because the shots made him feel "terrible." Said he: "It was one of the most fearful experiences of my life and I'd never go again." Tennessee Williams' brother says that the playwright spent three months in a mental hospital after Jacobson's treatments. Another patient, Photographer Mark Shaw, died of an overdose of amphetamines.

Stories of drug-dispensing "Dr. Feelgoods" have been part of medical folklore for some time and have occasionally surfaced in print. But none have been so startling as the *Times*'s

THE HISTORY OF DRUGS

Elvis Presley Received Drugs Without Prescriptions

Elvis Presley had an extensive drug abuse problem, including habitual consumption of amphetamines to give him energy. In addition to amphetamines, the famous singer abused other drugs apparently given to him by doctors to alleviate his chronic insomnia.

Prior to 1960, there is no evidence that Elvis was habituated to any sort of drug but benzedrine [an amphetamine], or amphetamine compounds. These pep pills had been part of his life since his first days on the road, and his use of them had continued straight through the period of his service in the army. Once he got back to Hollywood, however, he suddenly began consuming a whole range of drugs that produce narcotic and hypnotic as well as stimulant effects. How he first discovered and familiarized himself with these drugs is unknown; but, considering his later practices, it is very likely that he owed his introduction to these dangerous pills to the doctors to whom he complained of his inability to sleep.

Elvis was always an insomniac; now, under the stress of making movies and overstimulated by the constant use of Dexies [amphetamines] to get him going after nights with little or no sleep, he must have quickly approached that manic, round-the-clock sleeplessness that is typical of the speed freak. To one who believed that the solution to any problem of mind or body was a drug, nothing would appear more logical as an antidote to uppers than the use of downers. So, it is not surprising to learn that as soon as he became established at the Beverly Wilshire, he came to an understanding with a druggist at the Chrysler Pharmacy in the hotel lobby. This man began to supply Elvis with unlimited quantities of drugs without prescriptions at the price of one dollar a pill.

Soon Elvis was buying seven or eight thousand dollars' worth of pills at a time and paying for them by check.

Albert Goldman, *Elvis*. New York: McGraw-Hill, 1981.

disclosure. At least a dozen of the paper's reporters and researchers worked on the project [for] five months. Jacobson lost little time in defending himself and blasting what he termed "inaccuracies and distortions." He did not deny that at least some of his patients received amphetamines. Said he: "I have satisfied myself [that] in small amounts and [under] close supervision amphetamine can be a valuable tool in a doctor's hand." The dosages, he maintained, were "a good deal lower than those prescribed in the so-called, weight-reduction pills."

Moral Issue. The story raised some grave questions. Should the sanctity of the doctor-patient relationship be maintained even with Presidents, whose decisions can affect the safety, not to mention the survival, of the nation? Or should presidential prescriptions be made a matter of public record? Indeed, should doctors prescribe amphetamines at all? "If the case of Dr. Jacobson were unique, we would have only a small problem," says Dr. Willard Gaylin of the Institute of Society, Ethics and the Life Sciences in Hastings-on-Hudson, N.Y. "Unfortunately, it is not. Doctors round the country are still prescribing amphetamines massively, usually in the guise of weight control. But what they really do is give a lift."

Doctors may not be able to dole out such highs much longer. The American Medical Association regards amphetamine abuse as widespread and has asked all doctors to limit the drug's use to those conditions for which it is specifically indicated, such as narcolepsy (a condition characterized by brief attacks of deep sleep) and hyperkinesis (excessive activity) among children. The Federal Government may go even further. The Bureau of Narcotics and Dangerous Drugs has placed amphetamines on the list of controlled substances for which it sets manufacturing quotas. Studies now under way could lead to a reduction in these quotas.

A Diet Pill Addiction in the 1960s

Good Housekeeping

This selection from a 1967 issue of *Good Housekeeping* is a personal account written anonymously in the 1960s by a woman who began taking amphetamine diet pills in an attempt to lose weight after a pregnancy. In frustration, the new mother visited a physician and got a prescription for diet pills. The resulting weight loss, as well as the increased energy and euphoria she experienced on the pills, motivated her to continue taking them every day for the next five years. Eventually, the mother of three ended up in the hospital and came to the realization that she was indeed addicted to the diet pills. After a painful withdrawal from the amphetamines, she was able to recover.

Most women, I suppose, think of drug addicts as underworld characters. I know I used to. To me addicts were shadowy figures, huddling on street corners or darting into dark hallways, hypodermic needles in hand. Certainly I never dreamed that addiction could touch my own peaceful life.

But it did. And in the most painful way possible: I myself became addicted.

The drug wasn't heroin or morphine—nothing as sensational as that. It was one of those "innocent" drugs—a member of the amphetamine family—and it was given to me in the form of a diet pill. It was prescribed by a perfectly responsible physician at a time when I badly needed to lose weight. I lost the weight, all right, but kept on taking my pill—one a day, every day, for five long years—until, in the end, I was hooked. And, incredibly enough, I didn't realize what was happening until I'd almost destroyed my health, my marriage and my sanity.

Putting on Pounds

It all began with my first pregnancy. Up to then, I'd always watched my weight carefully. I had to; I seem to put on pounds just looking at a rich dessert. The minute I knew I was pregnant, though, I stopped counting calories. After all, I wasn't going to have a figure anyway; might as well enjoy myself— morning snacks, gooey desserts, peanuts, bedtime ice-box raids. And chocolates. Suddenly I had a craving for chocolates. I gained five—six—seven pounds a month. My doctor, a sweet old-fashioned type, never fussed about weight. As for my husband—Dave took for granted that naturally a pregnant woman gets fat: "She's eating for two."

All in all, I gained fifty pounds. The day I left for the hospital, I weighed 180, which is a lot to carry if you're five feet four!

Home from the hospital, I waited for the extra pounds to disappear. But I dropped to 160 and there I stuck. A size 18, and my husband liked slim girls! I didn't have any clothes that fit, and I certainly didn't want to buy any that size, so I mostly flopped around in dusters, feeling sorry for myself. And Roger was a colicky baby. Big and healthy, but how he did cry! Sometimes he howled from one feeding to the next. I was frantic. There was no time to think about exercise or diets. Even eating normally, I had scarcely enough energy to get through the day. Bending, lifting, pushing—everything was an effort.

Dave would come home late to find me still struggling with laundry, supper not ready. And if he was very hungry and tired, he'd ask, "What *do* you do all day?" Or—and this was hardest of all to take, "You know, if you lost a little weight, you'd move faster." I promised myself, "As soon as the baby settles down, I'll go on a diet."

Roger did settle down finally—but by then, wouldn't you know, I was pregnant again. At the same time, we moved (Dave's job as a professional forester takes him all over the country), so I had a different doctor.

Pills to Kill Appetite

This time there was no fatherly indulgence about weight. My new doctor took one look and was just plain horrified. "Young lady," he said, "you're at least 30 pounds too heavy. It's not good for you or for the baby. We'll have to do something." "I've tried to lose," I said. "But the more I think about dieting, the hungrier I get." The doctor nodded. "I know. But I can help you over the hump." He wrote out a prescription. "I want you to take one of these every morning. They may make you a bit jumpy, but they'll help you cut down on food."

As the doctor predicted, the pills killed my appetite, but as he hadn't predicted—and I hadn't dreamed of—they also gave me a tremendous lift. I'll never forget the feeling of that first pill. I'd popped it into my mouth and was warming Roger's bottle when it hit me. It was like an explosion in my head and my heart and my stomach—a happy-making, sparky excitement. The only time I had ever felt like that before was when I was stage manager in college for *Teahouse of the August Moon* and the director decided, a day before the show opened, that he wanted forty pillows dyed orange. That time, too, I went off like a rocket from a launching pad.

Now, instead of dragging about the house feeling fat and listless, I found myself bursting with energy. Cutting down on meals was no problem. Who had time to eat? Who cared about eating? A week after I started on diet pills I'd dropped five pounds and taken on a part-time job as a kindergarten teacher. I'd get up every morning, gulp my pill, and half an hour later I was wide awake, ready to go. Even six months pregnant, I was still active. I'd fix breakfast, take Roger to the baby-sitter, dash off to school, dash back at lunchtime, pick up Roger, feed him and put him down for his nap and then tackle the housework. I felt alive and wonderful. I ran the household efficiently, and I

THE HISTORY OF DRUGS

Amphetamines Used for Weight Loss

In the 1960s and 1970s, doctors prescribed a type of amphetamine called Benzedrine for weight loss. Those who took the pills found it easy to refrain from eating and enjoyed feeling happier and more energetic. These qualities of the drug contributed to the abuse of diet pills, which eventually caused side effects including insomnia, increased anxiety, and psychosis.

Of all the drugs prescribed for losing weight, benzedrine [an amphetamine] was by far the most appealing. It had few of the physical side effects and risks of thyroid or digitalis, and it did not flush out potassium and other nutrients as did the diuretics and the laxatives. It was psychologically satisfying, for it worked by making it easy to eat less and giving the illusion of increased willpower. It also made a person feel, at least for a few hours, happier and more energetic—an effect that made it a favorite of the pill-popping drug culture that had grown up in the late 1960s. So as digitalis, thyroid, and other weight-loss drugs were removed from the weight-loss arsenal, benzedrine—now usually referred to as amphetamine—came to be the drug of choice for many doctors trying to help patients lose weight.

But as their use grew, amphetamines' dark side came into view. Although people taking it did lose weight for a few weeks, their bodies quickly developed a tolerance for it. The weight loss—and the emotional highs—stopped, which led people to up the dose, trying to regain the magic of those first few weeks. . . . If the amphetamine use continued, the patient could expect insomnia, increased anxiety, and, in the long term, a psychosis much like paranoid schizophrenia. On the other hand, if the patient used amphetamine for a few weeks and stopped, the lost weight generally returned.

The FDA finally banned amphetamine in diet pills in 1979.

Robert Pool, *Fat: Fighting the Obesity Epidemic.* New York: Oxford University Press, 2001.

kept my weight down. A month after Joe was born, I was back to size 12, 130 pounds. Dave was thrilled. "It's certainly nice," he said, "to have a glamour girl around again."

Giving Up the Pills

I always took for granted that I'd give up diet pills when the baby came. Or did I? Anyhow, when we moved again, I took my prescription with me. I had no trouble getting it refilled. I was still taking a pill every morning. Never missed a day. If I was going to be away, even overnight, I carried my bottle with me. When we went on vacation, I made sure I had plenty of pills.

In the back of my mind, I suppose I was a little bit uneasy about my dependence on that daily tablet, and I'd begun telling myself that I'd give up the pills altogether—very soon. Some mornings I'd hesitate. "Maybe I won't take one today." But then I'd think "I have to go shopping," "I have to wax the kitchen floor," "I should make Roger a birthday cake. . . . Better take one." I could always find a reason.

Before Joe's first birthday I had another reason: baby number three was on its way. I couldn't risk zooming up to 180 again. When I went to the new doctor, I didn't tell him I was taking diet pills. I kept up my usual routine all through the pregnancy, and after it, too.

I'd begun to realize, though, that I was getting awfully irritable and jittery and to wonder if perhaps the pills were responsible. In fact, I'd almost made up my mind to give them up when we had a whole series of crises in the family. My mother died and Dad came to live with us. He needed a lot of attention just then and so did the baby and so did the boys. Also, it was forest-fire season. Sometimes Dave would get three or four fire calls a day; or be out all night and come home hungry for steak just when the kids were hollering for cereal and Dad was padding around the kitchen wanting his tea. Not the time to stop now, I figured. I needed all the energy I could muster.

But the pills didn't seem to be giving me quite the same lift they used to. I even considered increasing my dose. One day I took two.

The extra pill sent me high as a kite. My heart pounded, my whole body shook, and for the first time I was scared. What was in those pills? Why did I feel I *had* to have them? Could I possibly be—*addicted?* No, that was silly. I had a *prescription.*

I pushed the fears out of my mind and continued the diet pills. In February, 1966, I heard about a new law against refilling prescriptions calling for amphetamine. Did my pills, I wondered, contain amphetamine? I figured I'd better check on that—sometime. Then I read an article about dangerous diet pills, and the worry grew. According to the article, amphetamines (or "pep pills" as often called) were useful when cautiously administered for suppressing appetite as part of a medically supervised program. Abused, they might lead to hypertension, restlessness, rapid heartbeat, even hallucinations. Furthermore, prolonged use could result in addiction. Reading that article I had a pretty strong hunch about my own "pep pills." But I was only taking one a day. Surely *one* couldn't hurt me. And since I'd no trouble getting pills at the drugstore, they *had* to be okay. Besides, I could stop any time I wanted to—and I would, if I ever saw the need.

The warning of real trouble came in June [1966], five years after I started my daily pill routine. I began getting terrible cramping pains in my arms and legs. I'd wake up as tired as if I'd already walked ten miles. An hour on my feet, and I couldn't take the pain. I'd have to lie down. Mornings it was all I could do to get the boys dressed and fed before I collapsed on the couch. I had one infection after another, my head ached. The family doctor took X-rays and prescribed calcium tablets, but my pains got worse. I didn't mention diet pills to him, or to anybody.

Fear of Going Crazy

By this time I had a new, much worse fear: I felt that I was going crazy. There'd be weird memory lapses; I'd forget the name of someone I'd known for years. Or I'd be driving along in the car and suddenly not be able to remember where I was going. When people talked to me, I couldn't concentrate. My head went BUZZ BUZZ. Sometimes I felt all torn to pieces inside, but when I'd ask Dave, "Is my hand steady?" he'd say, "Sure." I screamed at the children for little things, or for nothing. Like one day Alec took a dollar bill out of the milk-money can and tore it into shreds. When I found him flushing the pieces down the toilet, I shook him so hard that he screamed and Dave charged in with, "Are you out of your mind?" Another time, while Dave was out fighting a fire, I sat down and wrote a note saying I'd decided to leave him. And by next morning, when he said, "What in heaven's name got into you?" I just didn't know. I couldn't remember.

In October [1966] I came down with gastroenteritis. I called the doctor, and he said to stop by the hospital. Since I thought it would just be for a shot, I didn't carry a thing with me. But the doctor took one look and put me in bed—in the hospital. There I was, with not so much as a pair of slippers—and no pills. Not that I thought about it at the time. I was so weak, with dehydration, virus and green-death all at once, that I could hardly walk. That was Saturday. For two days, I was groggy with sedatives. But by Monday night I more or less came to.

Climbing the Walls

Well, you hear about drug addicts climbing the walls when they need a fix. I know now what *that* means. I couldn't sit or lie down. I paced the floor, shaking. My head felt like it was separated from my body, just floating. Next morning, when Dave took me home, I thought I was flying apart. I went straight for my bottle and took a pill. Half an hour later, I was "normal" again. And then I knew for sure. I was hooked, as surely as if I'd been on heroin.

Finally I did what I should have done months before. I called the drugstore to find out what was in my pills. "Well," the druggist said, "they're a mixture. Dexedrine and Compazine." "Is that anything like amphetamine?" I asked. "You know, I've been taking them for years." There was a pause, and then the druggist said, "Compazine's a tranquilizer, to steady your nerves. Dexedrine is first cousin to amphetamine. It's a stimulant. You certainly shouldn't be taking those pills regularly unless you're under a doctor's care."

When I hung up, my hands were shaking, but I knew what I had to do next. I took my bottle of pills, drove to the doctor's, and told him the whole story. He was furious. "Do you realize," he stormed, "the harm you could do, dosing yourself with a powerful drug for five years? It's all very well to use amphetamines in the early stages of a diet as a kind of crutch. But you've been depending on them for a 'high,' for years. Let me tell you, you're lucky you got physically sick when you did. There've been cases where amphetamine addicts became so shot—mentally and physically—that they had to be hospitalized." "Not on one pill a day!" I protested. "Look," the doctor explained. "These things are relative. For some people, one pill a day might be a small dose. For you—well, look at the shape you're in. Obviously, that daily pill brought you close to complete collapse."

"What shall I do?" I asked.

"There's only one thing you *can* do. You're going off those pills right now. It won't be easy. I can give you sedatives that will help against withdrawal pains, but it's still going to call for every scrap of willpower you've got. There's a long hard fight ahead. And no one but you can win it."

A Long Hard Fight

Now, four months later, I know the doctor was right. For weeks after I gave up the pills, I felt like I was crouched at the bottom of a dark pit and couldn't get up the strength to crawl to the light. I'd get up in the morning with a cold inside me that no coffee was ever hot enough to reach. And I was weak, so weak

I couldn't make the bed. Dave would help me dress the boys and get Roger off to school. After that, I just lay on the couch shaking and crying. (I'd cry at practically nothing, or maybe I was really crying at everything.)

But, little by little, I've begun to pull myself together. Partly it has been Dave. I'd see him come home after a hard day, put on one of my aprons and make supper for us. Then he'd take the kids out for a ride so I could have a quiet time. And he's been so patient with my moods, and the fact that I haven't the strength to keep house. He used to complain when I didn't put his shoes away neatly. Now if he sees me picking up after the boys he says, "You go lie down. I'll do it." I worry about the weight I've gained—ten pounds since I went off the pills—but Dave says, "You look fine to me. Who wants to hug a coatrack?"

I know it'll be a long time before I've fully recovered from my five pep-pill years. But I am improving. My fits of depression come less often. Sometimes now I go a week without black moods. And when they come, they don't last so long. I've gone back to playing the piano—something I'd almost given up when I was on my pills, because music didn't give me pleasure then. It was like playing with gloves on. All my other responses are sharper now, too. It's as if I've been seeing things through frosted glass for a long time. Now I'm not, and I can see and reach out and touch.

Of course, I miss the pretty figure I used to have and all the extra zip the pills gave me. But I'm sure I'll get them both back without the help of drugs. Meanwhile, I figure I've already got something going for me: I know that I've got the willpower to see this business through and that willpower isn't something you can get from a pill bottle.

Speed Freaks of the Late 1960s

Edward M. Brecher and the Editors of Consumer Reports

This selection is excerpted from a Consumers Union report published in 1972 describing the development of intravenous (mainlining) amphetamine abuse in the United States. It also provides a profile of the speed freak of the late 1960s. It is believed that servicemen returning from the Korean War introduced the practice of intravenous amphetamine injection to this country. The practice spread alarmingly in the 1960s, with physicians and pharmacies making large profits from the irresponsible sale of what came to be called "speed." When law enforcement cracked down on legal sources for the drug, a black market flourished. Doctors reported that, initially, injecting speed was an ecstatic experience for young users because it alleviated depression and gave them a sense of confidence However, as they became addicted, they would inject amphetamines several times a day and stay awake for days at a time. Eventually, speed users could become malnourished, paranoid, psychotic, and prone to violent behavior. Speed freaks were generally white and middle class. They tended to lack criminal skills and were thus poorly adapted to the drug scene. Edward M. Brecher is an author and former editor for *Consumer Reports*, a magazine that provides product information, reviews, and ratings from experts.

Amphetamines taken orally can be used in excess with unfortunate results; but enormous quantities of oral amphetamines were consumed in the United States during the 1940s and 1950s with apparently little misuse. As late as 1963, indeed, the American Medical Association's Council on Drugs, while recognizing the possibility of misuse, reported that "at this time compulsive abuse of the amphetamines constitutes . . . a small problem [in the United States]." Much the same finding was reported from Sweden.

The intravenous injection of large doses of amphetamines, in contrast, is among the most disastrous forms of drug use yet devised. The early history of amphetamine mainlining has been explored by a California criminologist and authority on illicit drug use, Dr. Roger C. Smith, in an unpublished study he made available for this Report. Dr. Smith is now director of Marin Open House, a comprehensive center for drug and other problems in San Rafael, California. The Smith study was a part of the San Francisco Amphetamine Research Project, financed by the National Institute of Mental Health and launched by Dr. Smith in May 1968, in cooperation with the Haight-Ashbury Medical Clinic in San Francisco. Much of this [report] is drawn from Dr. Smith's study, "The Marketplace of Speed: Violence and Compulsive Methamphetamine Abuse," and from a report by a California psychiatrist, Dr. John C. Kramer, entitled "Introduction to Amphetamine Abuse," published in the *Journal of Psychedelic Drugs* in 1969. Dr. Kramer began his amphetamine research while he was on the staff of the California Rehabilitation Center in Corona, California—a center in which "speed freaks" as well as heroin addicts are incarcerated; he is at this writing on the faculty of the University of California at Irvine and on the staff of Dr. Jerome H. Jaffe's Special Action Office for Drug Abuse Prevention in Washington, D.C.

Early Intravenous Amphetamines

The earliest reference to the intravenous use of amphetamines that Dr. Smith was able to unearth concerned groups of American servicemen stationed in Korea and Japan during the early

1950s. These men were said to have learned to mix amphetamines—then nicknamed "splash"—with heroin and to inject the combination. This was, in effect, the traditional "speedball," with amphetamine substituted for cocaine. Servicemen brought the custom home with them after the Korean War. No doubt other small groups also learned to mainline amphetamine, alone or with heroin, during the 1950s; but no public furor was raised against the practice—and it did not spread alarmingly—until the 1960s.

[The nineteenth-century Austrian founder of psychoanalysis] Sigmund Freud's first dispensing of cocaine to a patient . . . was to help his pain-wracked friend, Fleischl-Marxow, get along without morphine. During the late 1950s, in the San Francisco Bay Area, a number of physicians prescribed amphetamine injections for the same purpose—or allegedly for the same purpose.

Dr. Smith reports there is little doubt that *some* Bay Area physicians were sincere in this use of amphetamines as a treatment for heroin addiction. They were nevertheless arrested for supplying drugs to heroin addicts. Other California physicians, it appears, were less conscientious. Some of them, for example, prescribed Methedrine (methamphetamine) "for heroin addiction" without even examining patients to see if they had needle marks. One Methedrine user told Dr. Smith:

> Then there was a doctor . . . who would write anything for anybody at anytime and he was making $7 a visit and on the day we went down there he wrote almost 400 prescriptions at $7 a head. So you can imagine how much money he was making. He made $2,800 that one day and they used to make caravans down there and even from [Los Angeles] to his place. You'd get within two blocks of his office and you'd start seeing people you knew from all over.

One heroin addict reported that for $6 or $7 he could get from one physician a prescription for 100 Methedrine ampules—plus hypodermic needles and sedatives. He could then sell enough of the ampules at $1 or $1.50 apiece to make a living. "In many instances," Dr. Smith adds, "heroin addicts who had formerly engaged in burglary, bad checks, credit cards, or a variety of other 'hustles,' began to make money exclusively by sales of Methedrine." It was at about this time, in the early 1960s, that Methedrine came to be known as "speed"—perhaps an allusion to its use in the traditional "speedball." More recently, "speed" has come to refer to *any* amphetamine which is injected intravenously.

In addition to the "scrip-writer" physicians described above, some San Francisco pharmacies began selling injectable amphetamines without a prescription, or on the basis of crudely forged prescriptions, or on a telephoned "prescription" from a user posing as a physician. Federal, state, and local law-enforcement agencies cracked down on such practices in 1962 and 1963; physicians and pharmacists alike were convicted of law violations, accompanied by widespread publicity. Thus the delights of amphetamine mainlining, previously known primarily to heroin addicts, became a matter of common knowledge and general interest.

The 1962 Amphetamine Scandal

When the injectable amphetamine scandal broke publicly in 1962, and federal and state agents descended on the manufacturers, [the pharmaceutical company] Abbott withdrew Desoxyn [methamphetamine] ampules from the market. In July 1963, Burroughs Wellcome similarly withdrew Methedrine ampules from distribution through retail pharmacies, but continued to make them available to hospitals as an adjunct to surgical anesthesia and for other essential uses. Withdrawal of legal supplies meeting FDA standards of purity for injectable products marked a turn for the worse. The black market next secured nonsterile amphetamines at trivial cost in vast quantity from large chemical manufacturing companies which shipped in bulk. The infection rate among addicts no doubt rose when these nonsterile products took the place of FDA-approved ampules.

Speed Labs

The 1962 crackdown on legal sources of amphetamines also triggered the emergence of illicit factories, called "speed labs," where speed was manufactured. "According to many of the users interviewed during the course of this study," Dr. Smith reports, "'speed labs' began to operate as early as 1962, and by 1963 several labs were in operation in the San Francisco Bay Area. Because of the shortage of speed in other cities on the West Coast [a shortage caused by the withdrawal of Burroughs Wellcome and Abbott ampules and by the crackdown on physicians and pharmacies], the manufacture and distribution of speed became an extremely profitable enterprise, and opened up new sources of revenue within the San Francisco drug scene.". . .

The Speed Run

The first use of intravenous amphetamine, Dr. Kramer notes, is "an ecstatic experience," and the user's first thought is, "Where has this been all my life?" Dr. Kramer goes on, "The experience somehow differs from the effects of oral amphetamines not only quantitatively but also qualitatively." After this first experience, the user mainlines intermittently for a time; "doses probably equivalent to twenty to forty milligrams per injection may be taken once or a very few times over a day or two. Days or weeks may intervene between sprees. Gradually the sprees become longer and the intervening periods shorter; doses become higher and injections more frequent.". . . "After a period of several months," Dr. Kramer continues, "the final pattern is reached in which the user (now called a 'speed-freak') injects his drug many times a day, each dose in the hundreds of milligrams, and remains awake continuously for three to six days, getting gradually more tense, tremulous and paranoid as the 'run' progresses. The runs are interrupted by bouts of very profound sleep (called 'crashing') which last a day or two. Shortly after waking . . . the drug is again injected and a new run starts. The periods of continuous wakefulness may be prolonged to weeks if the user attempts to sleep even as little as an hour a day.". . .

Enhancing Self-Image

Dr. Roger C. Smith here adds a highly significant fact about the intravenous-amphetamine euphoria. Many young people in our culture are brought up with a seriously damaged self-image. The methods of discipline imposed upon them as children, or other factors, convince them of their own inherent worthlessness, though they may mask this sense of worthlessness with bravado. "Many of the young people who are currently involved in the speed scene," Dr. Smith notes, "report that they were initially attracted to the drug because of the instant improvement noted in self-image. Many suffered from feelings of inferiority and lack of self-worth, which manifested itself in chronic, and often debilitating, depression.

"Many [of these young people with damaged self-images] had experimented with a variety of depressants, including heroin, barbiturates, and alcohol, but found that this only increased their feelings of depression and self-deprecation. The alleviation of depression brought about by the use of speed may well be the key factor in determining why *some* individuals progress from occasional to compulsive use of the drug"— though Dr. Smith also emphasizes that other factors may come into play as well.

In any event, Dr. Kramer points out, the improvement of self-image and relief from depression is purchased at a very high price if intravenous amphetamines are the mode of relief. Whether or not small oral doses of amphetamine are effective aids to dieting, the large doses taken during speed "runs" produce profound anorexia (lack of appetite). . . .

A paranoid psychosis, similar to the cocaine psychosis, is the almost inevitable result of long-term, high-dose, intravenous speed injection. This psychosis "can be precipitated by either a single large dose or by chronic moderate doses," Dr. Kramer adds.

Typical features of the speed psychosis include feelings of persecution, feelings that people are talking about you behind your back (delusions of reference), and feelings of omnipotence. Unlike paranoid schizophrenics, however, "speed freaks" are usually aware that these feelings are drug-induced; that is, they retain insight. [According to Dr. Kramer,] "High-dose intravenous users of amphetamines generally accept that they will sooner or later experience paranoia. Aware of this, they are usually able to discount for it." Nevertheless, Dr. Kramer adds, "when drug use has become very intense or toward the end of a long run even a well-practiced intellectual awareness may fail and the user may respond to his delusional system." Dr. Kramer cites others as believing that the drug merely brings into the open pre-existing paranoid tendencies. On the basis of his own experience with a large number of high-dose users, Dr. Kramer expresses the opinion, which he agrees is not testable, that despite differences in vulnerability to the paranoid effect, "anyone given a large enough dose over a long enough time will become psychotic.". . .

Profile of the Speed Freak

He is generally white, essentially middle-class in terms of education, family background and attitudes, and totally lacking in the kind of criminal skills which are essential to survival in a criminal environment. As critical as his lack of criminal skills is his failure to understand the values and norms traditionally associated with criminally oriented groups or subcultures. These values and norms are often antithetical to those of conventional society, but nonetheless they serve approximately the same function, namely, to offer guidance to participants and to control behavior which would be harmful to the group as a whole. . . .

While there is a backlog of experience and tradition which

the heroin addict in neighborhoods of high use can draw on, there is nothing similar in the speed culture, which emerged in its present form in late 1967, and is still undergoing rapid changes. Since there is little dependence on legitimate business for the exchange of merchandise for money, and very little integration with other illegal enterprises as one traditionally finds in heroin cultures, the "hustling" which does take place is sporadic, unskilled and predatory in nature, often directed toward fellow users and dealers, and only occasionally does it involve others outside the scene.

The speed freak is, in many ways, an outcast in a society of outcasts. He is regarded as a fool by heroin addicts, as insane and violent by those using the psychedelics or marijuana, and as a "bust" by non-drug-using hustlers.

Coming from a middle-class background, the speed freak attempts initially to support himself by "legitimate" means, "such as panhandling, selling underground newspapers, or working." But speed tends to incapacitate him for both legitimate employment and "hustling [according to Dr. Smith]":

> The compulsive speed user is usually incapable of hustles which demand composure, since he is highly agitated, suspicious and fearful that at any moment he may be detected, or the drug effect may leave him so paranoid that he would not take advantage of opportunities because they appear "too easy" or a "setup." Because of his compulsive verbalization, hyperactivity, emaciated physical state and bizarre demeanor, few businessmen will accept checks or credit cards from him. In our experience, many "speed freaks" who have attempted to pass bad checks have become panicked at a request for identification, convinced that his intended victim suspects him and will report him to police. In several instances, users have presented a check and immediately fled. . . .

Cut off in these ways from both licit and illicit employment, Dr. Smith continues, the speed freak survives by sponging on others and by dealing in drugs. Lacking skills and standards, he cheats. And the victims of his cheating are generally speed freaks like himself, paranoid like himself, on the verge of violence like himself. The violence that ultimately emerges—a high level of violence, including rape, mayhem, homicide—arises when the direct drug effect, the paranoia, occurs in a chaotic community where almost everybody is simultaneously engaged in sponging on everybody else, cheating everybody else—and suspecting everybody else. This is the scene that leads even confirmed drug users to conclude that "speed is the worst."

Recovering from Addiction

Contrary to a popular belief, however, speed—even in enormous doses—very rarely kills. Dr. Smith, for example, cites one case in which a speed freak injected 15,000 milligrams of the drug—15 full grams—in a twenty-four-hour period without acute illness. For neophytes, it has been stated, "death has followed rapid injection of 120 mg"; but "doses of 400 to 500 milligrams have been survived." "Very few deaths have been recorded in which overdose of amphetamines has been causal," Dr. Kramer declares.

That even massive doses of speed rarely kill is surely a tribute to the inherent toughness of the human body. That the human mind can ultimately recover even from prolonged amphetamine paranoia is an equal tribute to its toughness—yet that appears to be the case.

"What has been most striking in our experience," Dr. Kramer declares—and Dr. Smith agrees—"has been the slow but rather complete recovery of users who, according to their own descriptions and that of others, had become rather thoroughly disorganized and paranoid prior to their detention." The more florid symptoms fade within a few days or weeks. "Some confusion, some memory loss, and some delusional ideas may remain for perhaps six to twelve months. After that time, though there may be some residual symptoms, they are slight, and not disabling, and are noticed primarily by the (now abstinent) user himself. Most commonly, ex-users report slightly greater difficulty in remembering.". . .

Few Can Kick the Habit

The problem is how to achieve prolonged abstinence. Many speed users, like most of the heroin users, Dr. Smith notes, have tried repeatedly to stop by a conscious act of will. Few succeed. Their withdrawal misery is too great. "Many users who attempt abstinence find it difficult because of the fatigue which results, extreme at first, gradually diminishing but persistent, perhaps for months," Dr. Kramer adds.

Abstinence is often forced on a speed freak by a prison sentence, or by incarceration under a so-called civil commitment program, or by commitment to a mental hospital.

"No data has yet been collected to indicate the long-term value of such enforced abstinence," Dr. Kramer concedes; but on the basis of his own experience on the staff of the California Rehabilitation Center he is highly skeptical. "Certainly, many who have been incarcerated have returned to their drug use upon release." Thus the revolving-door pattern so familiar to heroin addicts may be the future of speed freaks as well. A person genuinely concerned for the welfare of speed freaks, Dr. Kramer sadly notes, is "in a bind. Users do not readily volunteer for care, but commitment programs offer little besides enforced abstinence. Should the user be permitted to live in the limbo of his drug or forced into the limbo of an institution? Can voluntary programs be devised which are sufficiently useful and attractive that users will seek them out and persist in their program? Can commitment programs be devised which do not resemble slightly benign prisons? Or, do we just let the user seek heaven or hell on his own terms while the community offers help only on its own terms?" Dr. Kramer poses these questions; neither he nor Dr. Roger C. Smith nor we have any glib answers to offer.[1]

---

1. Many methamphetamine treatment programs have been implemented since the 1970s. One of the most prominent, California's Centerpoint, requires many months of intensive outpatient rehabilitation as well as two years of aftercare. It requires two to three years of abstinence for the body to regenerate the destroyed dopamine cells in the brain. Because these cells are related to experiencing pleasure, the abstainer may have to suffer an average of two years of depression in order to recover.

CHAPTER TWO

Amphetamines in the 1980s and 1990s

The Controversy over Ecstasy in the 1980s

Kathryn Rose Gertz

In the next selection, Kathryn Rose Gertz describes the debate that took place in the 1980s over the dangers of MDMA, chemically related to amphetamines and commonly known as Ecstasy. At that time, Ecstasy was becoming the drug of choice, and reports of its widespread abuse led the Drug Enforcement Agency (DEA) to enforce a temporary emergency restriction on the drug. However, some pyschiatrists believed that because Ecstasy gives users an expanded capacity for self-awareness and an ability to share feelings, the drug could hasten the recovery of their patients. These psychiatrists therefore challenged the DEA's ruling, arguing that it would impede valuable medical research on the drug. Kathryn Rose Gertz is a journalist who has written for *Harper's Bazaar*.

Coeds pop it to party, singles call it the "hug drug," doctors swear that it sweeps away angst—and grateful patients agree. It is 3,4-methylenedioxymethamphetamine, or MDMA for short. Most, though, simply call it Ecstasy. Chemically, it is a made-in-the-lab concoction related to amphetamines, mescaline and a potent stimulant known as MDA. It is the hottest thing in the continuing search for happiness through chemistry. And now it is also illegal.

MDMA is not new. Developed back in 1914 by Merck as a diet pill but never manufactured, it was all but forgotten except for its inclusion in one army research project in 1953. Then in

Kathryn Rose Gertz, "'Hug Drug' Alert: The Agony of Ecstasy," *Harper's Bazaar*, vol. 119, November 1985, p. 56. Copyright © 1985 by *Harper's Bazaar*. Reproduced by permission.

the mid-1970s a few studies on the drug were published. Although there were no data recording its physiological effects, several psychiatrists began using it quietly as an adjunct to therapy—just the way they had originally handled LSD.

The pharmaceutical industry never produced MDMA commercially, and yet it was not banned. So there were always private chemists who would easily custom-make it for doctors and recreational users alike. Word quickly spread of its blissful benefits—advocates say it promotes intimacy, insight, empathy—and Ecstasy was on its way to becoming the drug-of-choice of the '80s.

Until the Drug Enforcement Agency [DEA] stepped in, that is. Last July [1985] acting on reports of "widespread" use and abuse, the DEA temporarily listed the drug as a Schedule I controlled substance, putting it in the same league as heroin, marijuana and LSD in order to "avoid imminent hazard to the public safety.". . .

Ecstasy's Therapeutic Value

Meanwhile, a group of psychiatrists, convinced of the drug's therapeutic value, have hired a lawyer to help them persuade the government to place it in the less restrictive Schedule III category. Unless this action is taken, they fear that the strictures will all but halt research, as evidenced by the fate of LSD when it was relegated to Schedule I in 1966.[1]

"The general properties of MDMA warrant a full exploration of this drug as a possible catalyst to insight-oriented psychotherapy," maintains Lester Grinspoon, M.D., professor of psychiatry at Harvard University and one of the doctors actively challenging the DEA. "Schedule III would give the DEA all the law and authority it needs to interdict production and prosecute possession, and at the same time would not compromise any clinical research." The DEA insists, however, that

---

1. As of May 2004, Ecstasy was still a Schedule I drug.

research will not be hindered, citing one FDA-cleared LSD project and the recent approval of THC (synthetic marijuana) for marketing.

"But that's not really the point," says DEA chemist Frank Sapienza. "We believe that MDMA does not fit the criteria for Schedule III. One requirement is that the substance have a presently accepted medical use, and we still do not believe it does. The other is that it have a relatively low abuse potential. We hold that it can be exploited based on its current clandestine production and widespread availability. All we have are anecdotal reports suggesting its role in therapy—and that's not enough."

The Case for Ecstasy

Indeed there are many favorable claims—both clinical observations and glowing testimonials from users. True, there is an initial 15 minutes or so when most experience varying degrees of sweating, jaw tightening, increased blood pressure and heart rate, nystagmus (involuntary eye movement), sometimes nausea. And afterward there are effects that may persist for 24 hours—exhaustion, appetite loss, sometimes sleeplessness. But enthusiasts contend that the four-hour duration of the drug's impact more than makes up for those fleeting discomforts. In addition, medical proponents insist that Ecstasy cannot be addictive because regular use nullifies the desirable, but not the negative, effects.

In interviews with three single women in their 30s—a flight attendant, a nutritionist and a trade journal editor—the reactions most commonly reported were self-acceptance, self-love, tolerance, contentment, tranquillity, insight and a consequent ability to unravel psychological knots. What's more, much of this equanimity seems to endure even after the drug has worn off.

Says the flight attendant: "It's as if you're living in a muddy pool and suddenly all the mud settles and the water is very clear. You can see everything so lucidly. I learned things about myself that I hadn't recognized before—like how self-critical I am. Now I'm less judgmental about myself and about others, too. I also used to be prone to mood swings. I won't say that will never happen again, but since taking Ecstasy I've been on an emotionally steady course. And I have learned to differentiate better between the important and the trivial. I'm sure that sooner or later these changes would have come about, but this just accelerated the process."

None of the three women expressed an overwhelming, overflowing kind of superelation as the chemical's name might suggest—just a "calm joy" as one of them put it. And they agreed with most every other account that the drug seems to take the sizzle out of sex; instead, most are content just to cuddle a lot. "I would not recommend it for people trying to get someone into bed," says the editor, "but I would for those trying to communicate better with others."

Then, too, at the "safe" dosage level of about 100 mgs. there is apparently no loss of self-control or any of the sensory pyrotechnics and other distortions associated with the psychedelic trip. Ecstasy is more subtle than that. "It offers," says Dr. Grinspoon, "a gentle invitation to introspection."

Psychiatrist Richard Ingrasci, M.D., who practices in Watertown, MA, and has administered MDMA to 200 patients since 1980, agrees. "It puts a person in an unbelievably open frame of mind," he says. "I've never seen anything like this in my 15 years of practice—the expanded capacity for self-awareness, the enhanced sensitivity, the increased ability to share feelings. All that's attributable, I believe, to the lowered fear and anxiety induced by this drug. I am not implying that this is a miracle, but it certainly can speed up therapy." Dr. Ingrasci adds that he has used the pill "successfully" with couples to break down the barriers between them; . . . with cancer patients to help them come to terms with death; and with those suffering from phobias, deep-seated childhood traumas and depression.

The Painful Price

"This is all very intriguing and worthy of further study, but it's simply a bunch of impressions," counters Ronald Siegel, Ph.D., an associate research professor in the department of biobehavioral sciences at the UCLA School of Medicine, who has testified in behalf of the DEA's position. "What about the rest of it? What about the sweating and nystagmus and jaw-tightening? The body is reacting with warning signals, trying to reject a foreign invader. Call it a psychological breakthrough, but recognize that you have slightly poisoned yourself." He is quick to point out that no one yet knows the toxicity level in humans. And there have been instances of abuse. The Haight-Ashbury Free Medical Clinic in San Francisco, for example, has reported abusers who have taken 10 to 15 doses at a clip.

Furthermore, the drug may cause long-term brain damage. Animal studies by Drs. Lewis Seiden and Charles Schuster of the University of Chicago—studies which the DEA used to support their emergency ban—show that MDA, a compound that differs only slightly from MDMA, "produces a marked depletion" of nerve cell chemicals involved in such basic functions as sleep, sex, mood, sensitivity to pain and aggression.

Their research also reveals that chemically similar methamphetamine can cause degeneration of cells that play a vital role in body movement. The damage is the same type that produces Parkinson's disease, the doctors say, although they note that it may take years for such problems to develop. "We are not yet exactly sure of Ecstasy's neurotoxic effects," admits Dr. Seiden, "but when very similar drugs demonstrate nerve cell death and potential disruption of key brain functions, it is likely that MDMA's consequences are equally serious. Until we have all the answers, we strongly discourage anyone from using it," he and his colleague warn. . . .

But even the pro forces concede one caveat. "Someone who thinks she is buying MDMA might be getting just about anything masquerading as Ecstasy," cautions one experienced researcher. "There is absolutely no such thing as quality control on the street. The range of misrepresentation is staggering. Using these drugs outside a doctor's office is like playing Russian roulette."

One chemical analysis confirmed that a capsule sold as MDMA contained only 57 mgs. instead of the paid-for 100 mgs. But the buyer of this dose may have been lucky. "We have reports from several cities that samples have been found to contain PCP," says UCLA's Dr. Siegel. Also known as Angel Dust, the compound can cause severe confusion and agitation. Dr. Grinspoon predicts that this sort of practice on the part of "illicit labs" will *increase* if MDMA is permanently classified as a Schedule I controlled substance.

Certain chemists may also fill the void with new "designer drugs,"—legal variations or analogs. Designer drugs are substances in which the psychoactive quality and intensity have been maintained, but the molecular structure has been altered slightly to skirt the law. The government may soon take action against this subterfuge, however. Right now [1985], Congress is considering a bill that would make it illegal to manufacture, distribute or possess such spin-offs.

Meanwhile, the Ecstasy controversy continues. "What I share with those who are enthusiastic about it is a desire to have chemical agents that may be useful in psychotherapy," says Dr. Siegel, who remains skeptical. "I believe that eventually these will be available—safely." But only research will tell if MDMA is the answer or just another false start in the pursuit of happiness.

"Ice" Addiction Reaches the United States

Michael A. Lerner

Hawaii was the first state in the United States to be afflicted by ice, a crystalline form of methamphetamine. This selection, written in 1989, describes the problem of ice abuse in Hawaii. The drug came to the islands from South Korea and by the end of the 1980s had become the state's most abused illegal substance. Ice was smoked by workers to help them stay more alert on the job and by recreational users to induce euphoria and a sense of well-being. However, the drug is as addictive as crack cocaine and its side effects—including fatal lung and kidney disorders as well as long-lasting psychological damage—can be devastating. Many authorities feared the spread of the drug to the continental United States. Indeed, in 1989, federal agents had already made several ice busts on the mainland. Michael A. Lerner is a journalist who writes for *Newsweek* magazine.

Twenty years old and fresh out of college, Tad Yamaguchi saw a good future for himself at an air-freight company in Honolulu. So when one of his superiors offered him a puff from the small glass pipe—a little something to help him get through the grueling 20-hour shift—Yamaguchi felt he couldn't refuse.

He says he was instantly hooked. "I felt alert, in control. It didn't seem to have a downside," recalls Yamaguchi. No wonder so many people in his office were using it. Four months later Yamaguchi, who had never done drugs before, was smoking every day. "I'd smoke as much as I could. I started buying large quantities to sell so I could support my habit," he says. Soon Yamaguchi, who kicked the habit a year ago, had lost 35 pounds and was smoking four days at a time, then "crashing" in a comatose sleep that lasted up to 36 hours. Next, paranoia and hallucinations set in.

The Japanese call it *shabu*, to Koreans it's *hiroppon*. To American addicts just discovering its intense highs and hellish lows, the drug is simply "ice," after the clear crystal form it takes in the manufacturing process. As addictive as crack cocaine but far more pernicious, ice—a type of methamphetamine, or speed—is a drug that seems culled from the pages of science fiction. In contrast to the fleeting 20-minute high of crack, an ice buzz lasts anywhere from eight to 24 hours. Unlike cocaine, which comes from a plant indigenous to the Andes, ice can be cooked up in a laboratory using easily obtained chemicals—a drug for the scientific age.

Methamphetamine's side effects are devastating. Prolonged use can cause fatal lung and kidney disorders as well as long-lasting psychological damage. "We're seeing people with dysfunctions two and a half years after they've stopped using. That's scary," says Earlene Piko, director of substance abuse at the Wai'anae Community Mental Health Center in Hawaii, the first American state to be afflicted by ice. The drug also tends to make users violent. The Honolulu Police Department estimates that ice was a factor in 70 percent of spouse-abuse cases the force handled last month.

Ice is not a new drug, but a more powerful form of a substance that has been popular in Western states for several years. Purer and more crystalline than the "meth" or "crank" manufactured in cities like San Diego, ice comes from Asia. So far, the spread to the United States has been largely confined to the Hawaiian Islands. But the quickness with which it has overtaken that state is startling. In just over four years, ice has surpassed marijuana and cocaine as Hawaii's No. 1 drug problem.

Korean Connection

Now law-enforcement officials fear Hawaii may be a beach-head for the drug's spread to the rest of the United States. Congresswoman Patricia Saiki of Honolulu has started lobbying drug czar William Bennett to declare her city a "high-intensity drug-trafficking area" so it would qualify for more federal anti-drug money. "[Bennett needs to act now] to quell this plague before it gets to the mainland," she says. It may already be too late. In recent months, federal drug and customs agents have made several ice busts in the continental United States.

Hawaii's ice trail goes back to South Korea, which—along with Taiwan—leads the world in the manufacture and export of the drug. The Koreans learned about methamphetamine from the Japanese, who invented the stimulant in 1893. During World War II, Japan's military leaders supplied it in liquid form to weary soldiers and munitions-plant workers, leading to the addiction of hundreds of thousands of Japanese to the then legal drug. Japan banned shabu in the '50s, but many labs that produced it simply relocated to South Korea and smuggled the drug back across the Sea of Japan. In recent years use has leveled off—though Japan remains the drug's largest market. At the same time, Korea's once negligible domestic consumption has boomed, spreading from prostitutes and entertainers to students, housewives and businessmen; 130,000 Koreans are addicted to ice, medical experts believe. A common factor among some users: jobs with high stress and long hours. "It's a very suitable drug for workaholics," says journalist Cho Gab Je, author of "Korean Connection," a book about the hiroppon trade.

The link between Korea and Hawaii was forged in the early

1980s through Paciano (Sonny) Guerrero, a Hawaiian of Filipino origins who last month was sentenced in Hawaii's federal court to 25 years in prison without parole for the sale and distribution of ice. Known as the King of Batu (the word for rock in the Filipino language of Ilocano), Guerrero established the first ice-distribution network on Hawaii, using mostly local Filipino gangs to distribute it. Authorities estimate that Guerrero sold $7.3 million worth of the drug in 1987 and 1988 alone. "Sonny was selling mainly to Filipinos and Koreans, but it quickly spread. And it's spreading still—right into middle-class high schools," says a Drug Enforcement Administration agent in Honolulu.

Gang Members

Korean drug organizations are trying to expand the ice market to mainland America. NEWSWEEK has learned that federal authorities are currently pursuing a Korean drug ring that is distributing ice in the United States. Last August, U.S. Customs agents in Portland, Ore., seized about five ounces of ice sent by mail from Korea. Last month Honolulu police arrested five suspected members of a violent New York–based Korean gang called K.P. (Korea Power) that allegedly arrived in Honolulu with 17 other gang members to set up an ice pipeline to the East Coast. Police seized $72,000 in cash along with guns and ammunition.

At first puff, ice seems irresistible. Cheap and long lasting, the drug provides users with a sense of well-being. A penny-size plastic bag called a paper costs $50 and, when smoked, can keep a novice high for up to a week. Addicts call the sensation from smoking ice "amping" for the amplified euphoria it gives them. Odorless and hard to detect, ice is used as much for recreation as for staying alert on the job. "On the front end, it doesn't seem so bad. You stay awake, focused on what you're doing. And you feel good about yourself," says Dr. Joseph Giannasio, director of Castle Medical Center Alcoholism and Addictions Program in Oahu. "Where it gets scary is at the tail end."

If Hawaii is any indication, a surge in ice use in America could be as destructive as the current crack crisis. Last month Honolulu Police Chief Douglas Gibb told Congress that the number of drug-exposed newborns reported to welfare officials has jumped from two a week to six a week in the past year. Ice largely accounts for the dramatic increase, say health experts, and the fallout is straining Hawaii's social services. "It's totally overwhelming. We're in a crisis," says Dr. Jane Stump, a psychiatry professor at the University of Hawaii and a member of the Child Protective Services medical team. "This ice, it's like a great tidal wave."

No Bonding

The little that is known about ice's effects on newborns is alarming. "If you thought cocaine dependency was bad, that's in the minor leagues compared to this drug," says Earlene Piko. As with cocaine babies, ice babies tend to be asocial and incapable of bonding. Some have tremors and cry for 24 hours without stopping. They have to be swaddled to be held. "We know children who didn't bond are likely to be sociopaths," says Daniel Bent, U.S. attorney in Hawaii. "We're now producing 200,000 cocaine babies a year, and nurses tell us ice babies are worse in that area."

Rehabilitation clinics in Hawaii report there are now as many ice addicts as cocaine addicts seeking treatment. Doctors believe it's just the beginning. "You have to build up a large base of users before you start seeing people come in for help," says Giannasio. Most clinics are treating ice addiction as they would cocaine addiction. But ice is proving more difficult to kick. "Some people get hospitalized, start on psychotropic drugs to stop the hallucination and after a month they're OK. But we have others who after two years haven't improved," says Piko. Honolulu police are preparing a number of public-service announcements to warn the population about the hazards of the drug. "We were ready for crack. We had commercials on TV, we learned how to bust the dealers and prosecute them," says Major David Benson of the Honolulu police. "But in its place, whammo, we got nailed with crystal meth." Federal authorities hope the continental United States won't face the same fate.

Toxic Meth Labs in the 1980s

Gordon Witkin

In the early 1980s simple recipes to produce methamphetamines contributed to the proliferation of illegal meth labs. In the following article, Gordon Witkin describes some of the hazards created by these labs, which sprang up all over the western United States. The major danger was the toxic waste generated by the production of methamphetamines. Operators of meth labs dumped their waste products down bathtub drains or along country roads and creeks, contaminating dwellings and polluting soil and water. Toxic by-products were also a threat to narcotics agents and police who were not equipped to handle them. The waste dump sites were not cleaned up because no one wanted to foot the bill. Consequently, lawmakers implemented a task force to create a comprehensive cleanup program. Gordon Witkin is a staff writer for *U.S. News & World Report.*

America's wicked romance with drugs has never been short on tragic consequences, from addiction and shattered lives to violence and death. Now [1989], as if there wasn't enough to worry about, authorities in the Western United States are adding a new problem to the list—hazardous waste.

Illegal drug labs set up in rented houses, motel rooms and remote forests are leaving a trail of tons of dangerous chemicals. So severe has the problem become in California that the state's emergency-response coordinator for toxic-substances control estimates that 70 to 80 percent of his calls now involve drug-lab waste. In December of 1986, toxic fumes from a suspected lab sent four people to a hospital and forced the evacuation of 50 nearby residents in San Mateo County, Calif. Last March [1988], more than 450 teachers and pupils were evacuated from a San Diego grammar school after chemicals apparently dumped by operators of an illegal lab were found to have leaked from drums and eaten away at the school playground. In Oregon, says Ed Wilson of that state's Department of Environmental Quality, "we have hunters finding containers of sludge in the woods and kids finding the stuff in vacant lots." The U.S. Drug Enforcement Administration (DEA) is spending some $5 million to $8 million annually to have private contractors haul waste from raided labs.

The root of the problem is methamphetamine, commonly known as speed, the use of which is spreading across the West like a wind-whipped brush fire. The off-white powder, usually inhaled or injected, is a powerful nervous-system stimulant with a high that lasts longer than that of cocaine.

"Meth" can be made with chemicals that have been easy to obtain and hardware that can be found in a typical high-school chemistry class. The growth of the meth market was spurred by development in the early 1980s of a shockingly simple recipe. Illegal labs have sprung up most dramatically in California, but notably also in states such as Texas, Oregon and Washington; seizures of labs by the DEA jumped from 122 in 1983 to 653 in 1987.

The chemical raw ingredients and the sludge by-products of the meth process add up to an environmental nightmare. They range from toxic substances such as hydrogen-chloride gas and lead acetate to explosive and inflammable materials such as ether and red phosphorus. The meth "cookers," says one California DEA agent, "aren't going to call a legitimate disposal company to haul off their waste." Instead, they dump gallons of the stuff wherever they please—down bathtub drains, in backyard pits and along roads and creeks, contaminating dwellings and polluting soil and water.

Hazard to Narcotics Agents

The wastes are not only a serious long-term problem but also an acute hazard to narcotics agents who carry out raids on the labs. "We're cops, not environmental experts," is a common refrain. In mid-1987, the DEA instituted courses for its agents on the hazards of meth labs and started issuing them protective suits for such encounters. Many state and local police agencies, however, still don't have the necessary training or equipment to safely deal with the labs.

Adding insult to possible injury, the enforcement agencies find that raiding a lab can make them responsible for its waste. The Environmental Protection Agency (EPA) even ruled that the DEA is technically the "generator" of meth-lab waste that it discovers, making it legally liable for the cleanup.

At the state level, deciding who's going to clean up and who's going to pay often becomes a jurisdictional black hole of finger pointing and buck-passing. The result, asserts Dan Largent of the California Justice Department's Bureau of Narcotics Enforcement, is that "we've got sites all over California that are infected with hazardous and toxic waste from drug labs that have never been cleaned up."

Addressing the Problems

In an attempt to address some of those problems, Representatives Robert Dornan (R-Calif.) and Ron Wyden (D-Oreg.) successfully pushed for creation of an EPA-DEA task force on illegal drug labs as part of the massive 1988 drug bill signed last fall. The task force will strive to counsel local agencies, iron out this panoply of jurisdictional hassles and implement a comprehensive cleanup program.

Many in enforcement believe that the best way to cut into

the meth market and the waste it produces is to restrict sales of the so-called precursor chemicals used to make methamphetamine. Several states now require dealers to get permits to sell these chemicals and keep records of exactly who's buying them. Congress put similar record-keeping requirements in last fall's drug law.

Narcotics cops are encouraged by all that, but with meth traffickers it's still a cat-and-mouse game. Many of the chemicals cannot be outlawed entirely because they have legitimate uses. Traffickers also stay ahead of lawmakers by creating new recipes that use slightly different precursors not covered by existing legislation. All of which means that controlling methamphetamine, like other battles in the drug war, is likely to be a long, often depressing fight, only this time with an additional victim: The environment.

Mexican Methamphetamine Trafficking Organizations of the 1990s

Randy Weaver

Randy Weaver is a senior research specialist at the National Drug Intelligence Center. The following selection is taken from a speech he delivered at the National Methamphetamine Drug Conference in May 1997. In the 1990s, Weaver explains, Mexican methamphetamine organizations became powerful and brought the illicit methamphetamine market to a higher level of sophistication. He describes how large methamphetamine labs were run in both Mexico and the United States and how the drug was transported and distributed from the labs. Many Mexican lab operators conducted their drug transactions on a cash-only basis because they were distrustful of banks and wanted to avoid creating any incriminating records. Although the southwestern United States was initially the core area for large Mexican drug lab operations in the 1990s, the labs rapidly expanded into other parts of the United States.

Mexican organizations produce methamphetamine using the ephedrine-reduction method [using bulk ephedrine powder],

Randy Weaver, speech at the National Methamphetamine Drug Conference, May 28, 1997.

the best-known way to clandestinely manufacture bulk quantities of methamphetamine. There are three essential chemicals required for this method of methamphetamine production: Ephedrine or pseudoephedrine, hydriodic acid and red phosphorous.

Mexican organizations have managed to remain steps ahead of law enforcement in developing and maintaining sources of supply for both ephedrine and pseudoephedrine. They have answered every attempt at regulation with an almost immediate shift to an alternate source. While regulatory efforts have clearly reduced the domestic availability of ephedrine and have had some success in reducing overseas availability, the largest Mexican organizations have little difficulty obtaining bulk quantities of ephedrine.

The primary source countries for ephedrine and pseudoephedrine have fully cooperated with U.S. international control efforts. Mexican methamphetamine organizations have maintained access to bulk supplies of ephedrine and, most recently, phenylpropanolamine [an ingredient used in prescription and over-the-counter drug products as a nasal decongestant and in weight control products to control appetite], by resorting to smuggling via mislabeled shipments. Despite attempts to control the commerce in pseudoephedrine and ephedrine, China and India have increased production in [the 1990s], increasing the likelihood of illegal precursor shipments. During 1995 and 1996, smuggled shipments from Taiwan and the United States provided phenylpropanolamine to some of these drug traffickers, which they used to replace reduced supplies of ephedrine.

Multimillion Dollar Trade in Pseudoephedrine

Many Mexican organizations operating laboratories in the United States have turned to pseudoephedrine as a substitute for bulk ephedrine. These labs are supplied with tens of millions of pseudoephedrine tablets per month by rogue chemical companies, many of which do little-to-no business with the retail drug business or the health care industries. These individuals operating networks of liquor stores and convenience stores are the primary conduit through which pseudoephedrine reaches many domestic methamphetamine laboratories. The illicit trade in pseudoephedrine is, in itself, a multimillion dollar annual industry.

The historical trends identified for ephedrine and pseudoephedrine also applied to hydriodic acid, but, more recently, trends indicate hydriodic acid is no longer the critical commodity it has been in the past. Because of the difficulty of obtaining and transporting large quantities of hydriodic acid and its increased price, many organizations now add the necessary ingredients to the reaction process, allowing hydriodic acid to be produced as methamphetamine is synthesized.

Some Mexican organizations establish front businesses to provide large-scale procurement of precursor chemicals. Others establish networks of individuals to accomplish that function. These networks use numerous automobiles and disposable individuals know as runners. Runners will purchase chemicals from any company that will sell to them, including some on the East Coast and in Midwestern states. These networks are usually established by larger organizations that specialize in bulk methamphetamine production.

Mexican Labs in the United States and Mexico

The largest Mexican organizations have production operations in both the United States and in Mexico, but domestic labs differ greatly from labs in Mexico that are usually larger and more secure facilities than those in the United States. Labs in Mexico generally produce far more methamphetamine than labs in the United States, sometimes as much as 150 to 200 pounds per cook performed every other day. By contrast, Mex-

ican organizations in the United States typically maintain
three to seven locations that can be used as clandestine lab

THE HISTORY OF DRUGS

Chemical Supplies in
Methamphetamine Production

*Chemicals needed for the production of methamphetamines
were supplied to Mexican traffickers by Czech, Indian, and
Chinese manufacturers in the early 1990s.*

Beginning in 1990, new U.S. laws drastically reduced the
availability of chemicals from domestic sources which are
needed for methamphetamine production. By 1992, traffickers
in Mexico had identified foreign sources of supply which
would be imported directly into Mexico for the manufacture of
methamphetamine, which was then smuggled into California.
The sources were major legitimate manufacturers in the
Czech Republic, India and China who were selling to brokers
in Switzerland and other countries, who, in turn, arranged for
transportation to Mexico. Traffickers from Mexico were able to
import over 170 metric tons of ephedrine in little over a year.
This quantity would make approximately 140 metric tons of
methamphetamine.

Simultaneously, traffickers discovered a loophole in the
U.S. law. Although controlling ephedrine and pseudoephedrine as chemicals, it did not extend to pills which
contain these chemicals. West Coast methamphetamine traffickers discovered that they could order hundreds of pounds
of these tablets from mail order supply houses most of which
were located on the East Coast. DEA [Drug Enforcement
Agency] investigations have shown that many of these suppliers were well aware of the purpose for which these pills were
being purchased. In a single case involving a company in
Pennsylvania, records showed that almost 91 tons of pills
were sold to traffickers in less than two years.

Thomas A. Constantine, congressional testimony given before the House
Crime Subcommittee, October 26, 1995.

sites when necessary. Since chemicals and equipment are frequently removed from U.S. lab sites after a cook, U.S.-based cooks usually average only 10 to 15 pounds of methamphetamine per cook, significantly less than the operations in Mexico. Lab operations in the United States for non-Mexican organizations are significantly lower in terms of production capabilities.

Although that trend seems to be continuing, larger lab sites capable of producing more than 200 pounds of methamphetamine have been located in the United States. Labs in Mexico are often located on a family-owned ranch, farm, residence, or in a business. In the United States, labs may be located in an auto body shop, an abandoned mine, a deserted trailer or outbuilding, an apartment, a hotel room or in an orchard. The location of a lab site frequently depends upon the preference of the cooker, but, wherever the lab may be located, one fact remains absolutely constant: Five to six pounds of toxic waste are generated for every pound of methamphetamine produced at a clandestine lab site.

Once a lab site is located and established, organization leaders select personnel who will participate in the manufacturing operation. Methamphetamine manufacturing depends upon persons performing four specific roles. The manager of the entire manufacturing operation is the lab foreman, who is usually a cook himself and a highly-trusted member or leader of the organization. The cooker is also a trusted and usually experienced individual who oversees the actual manufacturing process. The cooker instructs and supervises the lab workers but personally performs the more sensitive tasks of mixing and heating the chemicals.

The least trusted individuals involved in the manufacturing process are the lab workers. They perform the physical labor and hazardous tasks associated with manufacturing methamphetamine. Security personnel are usually trusted individuals who safeguard the lab site from the other organizations and law enforcement. Security personnel also maintain watch over the lab workers and prevent them from leaving the lab site until the cooking process is complete.

Ideally, these four roles are filled by individuals from the same organization; this affords the greatest measure of security and cooperation but also results in a greater profit margin for the organization. This self-sufficient style of manufacturing methamphetamine is the goal of emerging methamphetamine organizations. While there are many cookers producing methamphetamine, only a few cookers actually possess the skill to supervise a large cook of more than 50 pounds, ensure a high-purity product and train other cookers.

These highly-skilled cookers are frequently associated with more than one production and distribution organization and often work in labs in both the United States and Mexico. Mid- to low-level Mexican methamphetamine organizations frequently exchange cookers, lab sites, precursor chemicals, and at times, even methamphetamine, but they are still very dependent upon a continuous supply of precursor chemicals.

Couriers Transport Methamphetamines

Mexican organizations use couriers who are trusted individuals, family members, or close family friends to move methamphetamine. Couriers associated with lab facilities in Mexico frequently smuggle both methamphetamine and ephedrine into the United States and often carry cash back into Mexico. The transportation of precursor chemicals and methamphetamine into Mexico is dependent upon the same methods, routes, individuals and organizations that have historically moved other contraband through Mexico.

The preferred method of transporting precursor chemicals and methamphetamine is the automobile. These automobiles are frequently equipped with electronically-activated compartments to conceal drugs or chemicals. When transporting contraband in this manner, couriers attempt to avoid any identifiable patterns of behavior. To transport especially large loads of methamphetamine, Mexican organizations have used both tractor-trailer rigs and even private aircraft. To transport smaller amounts of methamphetamine, Mexican organizations will use mail services. The U.S. Postal Service, United Parcel Service and Federal Express have all been used to transport both methamphetamine and cash. The use of mail services allows for easier expansion of distribution to developing market areas outside the Southwestern United States, which remains the core area of operations.

Mafia Prison Gangs Distribute Meth

Finished methamphetamine is frequently uncut until it reaches street-level distributors. Our analysis revealed an average purity level of 80 to 90 percent for even small amounts of methamphetamine, indicating that the responsibility or necessity of cutting methamphetamine rests with street-level distributors. The Mexican Mafia prison gang plays an important role in methamphetamine distribution, especially in Southern California and Arizona. The Mexican Mafia provides a connection to street gangs that methamphetamine production organizations can exploit. With established distribution throughout their ranks, outlaw motorcycle gangs are another important distribution connection for Mexican organizations.

Historically, demand at the wholesale level drove the production of methamphetamine, with demand known and quantities and pricing negotiated before methamphetamine was manufactured. Recent methamphetamine seizures indicate the trend may be changing. Seizures of multi-hundred-pound quantities of methamphetamine and reports of methamphetamine warehouses suggest the larger Mexican organizations may be surpassing traditional demand-driven production requirements.

Unlike their Colombian counterparts, mid- to upper-level leaders of Mexican methamphetamine organizations may be personally involved in both production and distribution. Leaders of Mexican organizations seem to prefer a more direct measure of control over every aspect of their operations. Many leaders have worked their way up the scale from street-level distribution to leadership within the organization.

Lab Leaders Operate Only with Cash

Sophisticated, structured laundering of drug proceeds, as practiced by many drug trafficking organizations, is quite rare in Mexican methamphetamine organizations. Mexican meth-amphetamine organizations do not typically attempt to make drug proceeds appear legitimate through structured deposits and wire transfers. The leaders of Mexican methamphetamine organizations prefer instead to hold their money in cash form or invest in real property. Mexico-based organizations continually transport large sums of cash from the United States to Mexico. Because of their distinct distrust of banks and other financial institutions, leaders of methamphetamine organizations in the United States and Mexico may hide large sums of cash in secure locations, often going as far as burying containers full of millions of dollars in cash.

Directly corresponding to their preference to possess cash, leaders of Mexican organizations also prefer to conduct business transactions in cash, even very large transactions. This method of cash exchange affords them a greater degree of security and simplicity and eliminates any potentially exploitable record of criminal activity.

While their preference to possess cash and conduct business in cash terms is simple and difficult to track, it presents Mexican organizations with a significant logistical challenge, the movement of the cash itself. Larger Mexico-based organizations may move hundreds, even thousands of pounds of cash per year. And since most large cash transactions are still performed in Mexico, continuous operations depend heavily upon the physical movement of tens and, at times, hundreds of thousands of dollars in cash per trip.

Although our initial analysis focused almost entirely on the Southwestern United States, some recent trends in methamphetamine manufacturing and distribution have become apparent. Methamphetamine abuse has become a rapidly-expanding phenomenon of national proportions that poses a major threat to our economy, our society and to the environment.

The number of labs seized in the United States has risen dramatically in the [mid-1990s]. Though smaller [mid-1990s] labs not directly associated with the Mexican organizations may outnumber Mexican labs numerically, they cannot compare with the volume of methamphetamine and, correspondingly, the volume of toxins produced by Mexican organizations.

Current State of Mexican Organizations

Mexican organizations have generally supplanted outlaw motorcycle gangs in methamphetamine production and now use outlaw motorcycle gangs to facilitate their distribution activities. Couriers for Mexican organizations now routinely use domestic commercial airlines to expand distribution to new market areas. There are strong indications that the larger Mexican methamphetamine organizations are supported by even larger organizations like those led by the Arellano-Felix brothers [Mexican drug cartel] and Amado Carrillo-Fuentes [powerful Mexican drug trafficker who died in July 1997]. Our analysis and recent discussions with law enforcement personnel at federal, state and local levels indicate the preeminent Mexican methamphetamine organizations are undergoing a systematic expansion to areas well beyond their core area.

In summation, the incursion of Mexican methamphetamine organizations into the illicit methamphetamine market has added a level of organization, sophistication and scope that were not the case before their ascension. Mexican organizations now comprise a major portion of the methamphetamine threat to the United States.

Speed Is the Drug of Choice for Pregnant Women in the 1990s

Marilyn Kalfus

In the mid-1990s pregnant women in the United States abused methamphetamines, also known as speed, more than any other drug. In the next article, Marilyn Kalfus describes some of the dangers for babies born to mothers addicted to speed, including premature birth, malnourishment, agitation at noise or light, inconsolability, and possible brain hemorrhaging. The babies were also at high risk of developing attention deficit disorder and behavioral problems. In addition, because many of the addicted mothers were not considered capable of caring for their newborns, the babies were given to relatives to be nurtured or were put into foster care. Marilyn Kalfus is a staff writer for the *Orange County Register* in California.

Tammy Wright remembers snorting methamphetamine while she was pregnant with two of her daughters. But she has only a faint recollection of being warned that the drug could pose a danger to her unborn children.

"If I did hear it," says Wright, 25, whose meth problem ultimately cost her custody of the two little girls and an infant daughter, "I didn't hear it."

Health officials say methamphetamine, also known as speed or crank, has become the drug of choice among pregnant women, often hooked before they realize that they're smoking, snorting or slamming for two.

Short-Term Effects on Newborns

The short-term effects on newborns who were exposed or addicted to the drug mimic those of cocaine: premature birth, inconsolability, irritability, malnourishment, feeding problems, agitation at any noise or light. Some babies vomit or claw at themselves. There's also the risk of a brain hemorrhage.

Doctors say it's too early to tell what the long-term effects will be.

"These are the kids who will be more likely to develop attention deficit disorder and have more social and neurobehavioral problems," said Dr. Vicki Darrow, medical director of the Perinatal Substance Abuse Services program of Orange County, Calif.

But mothers who've kicked their meth habits say they never focused on the future.

"When you're high, you're not even considering that," Wright said. "The drugs got you in a totally different state of mind."

Two years ago [in 1994], heroin appeared to be the most pervasive illegal drug among pregnant mothers in treatment, Darrow said, but meth has edged it out.

When 120 women in the program were questioned about their drug of choice [in 1995], 36 percent named methamphetamine, 34 percent heroin, 11 percent cocaine, 9 percent marijuana, 7 percent alcohol and 3 percent other drugs, she said.

Other studies of pregnant women on drugs do not break [down] individual substances, and local and state agencies did not have figures for the numbers of babies born exposed to or addicted to speed. But doctors and health-care workers at Southern California hospitals say they're seeing more pregnant women on methamphetamine—and more babies in neonatal units because of the drug—than in the past.

No Way to Quantify the Problem

"You can't just universally screen people (for drugs). There's no way to quantify the problem," said Dr. Jack Sills, medical director of the neonatal intensive care unit at University of California Irvine Medical Center. But, he said, "We know it's there."

When an infant's urine screens positive for drugs, "More than likely, it's speed," said Melissa Gleason, a social worker at Martin Luther Hospital Medical Center in Anaheim. "Most of the (drug-using) moms that I see have used methamphetamine."

"Speed is better than cocaine," said Tina Greathouse-Gonzalez, who injected methamphetamine and also took heroin and cocaine while she was pregnant with her son Joseph. He's now 5 months old and "perfect," she says, despite weighing 4 pounds at birth.

"With coke, you can't get enough," said Greathouse-Gonzalez, 28, of Anaheim. "It (speed) lasts longer."

Meth Trends in the California Population

The trend mirrors what is happening in the general population: Methamphetamine abuse in Southern California has become an epidemic that's sending twice as many users to emergency rooms, setting a record for the largest single-year increase in ER admissions recorded for an illegal drug in California, according to a recent study by the Public Statistics Institute of Irvine.

Hospital admissions for meth abuse in California went from 6,817 in 1993 to 10,167 in 1994. Orange County admissions were up 67 percent from 1993 to 1994, when there were 662 such emergency-room visits, according to the study. Ten years earlier, there were only 86.

Law-enforcement agents closed down 13 suspected meth labs in Orange County in 1992, 26 in 1994 and 41 in 1995, and narcotics agents estimate they'll close down 100 this year [1996].

[In July 1996], California Gov. Pete Wilson introduced the Infant Health and Protection Act, which would require county social workers to intervene any time a hospital discovers a newborn exposed to illicit drugs. Currently, a positive toxicology test is not enough, in and of itself, to qualify as child abuse or neglect. Under the proposed law, infants would be allowed to go home only if the mother complies with drug monitoring.

The rationale is that such youngsters eventually will wind up in the system, anyway.

What Meth Does to the Unborn

Doctors say methamphetamine constricts the mother's blood vessels, cutting off nutrients to the fetus. A meth binge also can bring on constrictions that separate the placenta from the wall of the uterus prematurely and push the baby out weeks too soon.

"We just know these type of stimulants are strong vaso-constrictors. You always wonder what it's doing to the (baby's) brain," Sills said.

The brain hemorrhage that a meth baby can suffer is potentially more serious than ones in ordinary preemies, Sills said, because it strikes in the white matter, and ultimately could result in a spastic condition.

"Speed's worse (than other drugs) when you're pregnant, because you don't eat or sleep at all," said Greathouse-Gonzalez, who, at 5 feet 2 inches tall, said she weighed 90 pounds—almost 50 pounds less than she does now—during her pregnancy. "It (the unborn baby) is not getting nothing."

But doctors say a fetus can be resilient, and some newborns exhibit no immediate effects.

Others get overstimulated too easily.

"Lights may be really, really bright to this baby," said Joan Baran, an infant psychologist at Children's Hospital of Orange County. "If you lower the light intensity, they calm down."

Psychologists counsel mothers not to touch and talk to these babies simultaneously, so as not to overload the infants' senses.

Otherwise, said Baran, "If a mom is not able to recognize some of the difficulties the child is having, the woman feels rejected by her baby."

Mothers Hide Their Drug Addiction

But some mothers never seek help. They try to hide their history of drug use, get through the delivery and bring the baby home without a hassle.

"There are a significant number of these mothers who absolutely know the system," said Dr. Leonard Fox, neonatal director at Martin Luther Hospital Medical Center. "They know what to say, that they haven't taken any drugs in the last six months. They will tend to not deliver at the hospital where they had their prenatal care. For example, the mother will live in San Bernardino but be 'visiting a friend in Orange County' when they go into labor."

Kathleen Johnston, seven months pregnant, figures she was snorting or smoking meth—or putting it in her coffee—every day around the time she got busted for violating her probation earlier this year. She'd been placed on probation after a one-year jail term for selling meth.

Johnston, who said she learned she was pregnant only after she was back in jail on the probation violation, says she's glad she got caught, because it forced her to go clean.

"I probably would have lost the baby, or the baby would've been born addicted," said Johnston, of Stanton, Calif., in a jailhouse interview. "I was hooked on it."

Who Cares for the Babies

Fox said the courts try not to take babies away from new mothers, which could mean sending the infant home with another relative instead of removing the newborn from the family.

"The mother still gets to be with the baby," he said. "That's probably the best way. You don't want to break up that bond."

Greathouse-Gonzalez, who took heroin and cocaine shortly before she went into labor with Joseph ("I slammed, and all of a sudden the water broke," she says) lost the newborn temporarily. Under court order, he was placed in Orangewood Children's Home, then in foster care.

"I straightened up right then," she said. She'd already given up a son, born two months early and weighing 3 pounds, to adoption nine years ago. She'd been taking drugs then, too, she said.

Wright, of Garden Grove, Calif., has been straight for 16 months and has a 6-week-old daughter. But she wonders what has become of her three other girls, who were put up for adoption at ages 3, 2, and 3 months, after Wright went on a meth binge that left her so gaunt the 5-foot-3-inch woman had to wear child-size clothing while her youngsters sometimes went dirty and unfed.

"I know there's probably some developmental effects on each of them as they get older," she said of the two girls exposed to methamphetamine during her pregnancies.

Doctors have told her that her second daughter, born prematurely, was coming along at a slower rate than she should have been.

"Had I not used," Wright said, "she would not have been premature."

When Wright finally sought treatment, she said, "Every single (pregnant) woman in my class, their drug of choice was speed."

Said Wright, "A lot of girls have a weight problem, and it helps you to lose weight. They usually started before they were pregnant. By then it's got control of you. You can't think straight."

CHAPTER THREE

Amphetamines Today

An Overview of the Methamphetamine Problem in America

Rogelio E. Guevara

Methamphetamine is relatively easy to manufacture. This fact, as well as the availability and low cost of the chemicals needed to produce the drug, has contributed to epidemic abuse of methamphetamines. According to official reports, more than nine thousand meth labs were seized in the United States in 2002. Most of these labs were small toxic labs that produced ounce quantities of methamphetamine for local use. These small operations accounted for 95 percent of clandestine lab seizures. In addition, Mexican labs produce enormous quantities of the illegal drug and are major suppliers of methamphetamines to the United States. The Drug Enforcement Administration (DEA) is pursuing measures to eliminate Mexican trafficking organizations as well as the smaller labs. In the following selection, Rogelio E. Guevara describes different aspects of the methamphetamine problem in the United States. Guevara is chief of operations of the Drug Enforcement Administration of the U.S. Department of Justice.

According to the 2001 National Household Survey on Drug Abuse, over nine million Americans or 4.3 percent of the United States population reported having tried methamphetamine on at least one occasion during their lifetimes. The Drug

Rogelio E. Guevara, testimony before the House Committee on Government Reform, Subcommittee on Criminal Justice, Drug Policy, and Human Resources, Washington, DC, July 18, 2003.

Abuse Warning Network (DAWN) estimated that the number of emergency department episodes concerning methamphetamine increased from 10,447 in 1999 to 14,923 in 2001.

In 2002, the El Paso Intelligence Center (EPIC) reported the seizure of over 9,000 clandestine methamphetamine laboratories. Additionally, in the "Associated Children Report" for 2002, EPIC reported over 2,000 children were present during the seizure of these laboratories. Of this total, 1,382 children were reported as having been exposed to toxic chemicals. These figures concerning the abuse of methamphetamine, seizure of clandestine methamphetamine laboratories and the presence of children at the lab sites, clearly demonstrate that many parts of America are indeed in the grasp of methamphetamine.

About Methamphetamine

Methamphetamine is a synthetic central nervous system stimulant that is classified as a Schedule II [see Drug Schedules in Appendix] controlled substance. It is widely abused throughout the United States and is distributed under the names "crank", "meth", "crystal" and "speed". It is commonly sold in powder form, but has been distributed in tablets or as crystals ("glass" or "ice"). Methamphetamine can be smoked, snorted, injected or taken orally. The clandestine manufacture of methamphetamine has been a concern of law enforcement officials since the 1960's, when outlaw motorcycle gangs produced their own methamphetamine in labs, and dominated distribution in the United States. Clandestine labs typically produce other types of illicit drugs such as PCP ["angel dust"], MDMA [Ecstasy], and LSD, but methamphetamine has always been the primary drug manufactured in the vast majority of drug labs seized by law enforcement officers throughout the nation. Since 1997, 97 percent or more of the clandestine lab seizures reported to DEA [Drug Enforcement Administration] were either methamphetamine or amphetamine labs.

Methamphetamine is, in fact, a simple drug to produce. After being introduced to the drug, many abusers learn that methamphetamine can be manufactured using common household products found at department and hardware stores. These ingredients are not only readily available, but also inexpensive. For approximately $100 in materials, a "cook" can produce $1,000 worth of methamphetamine. Items such as rock salt, battery acid, red phosphorous road flares, pool acid, and iodine crystals can be utilized to substitute for some of the necessary chemicals. Precursor chemicals such as pseudoephedrine can be extracted from common, over-the-counter cold medications. A clandestine lab operator can utilize relatively common items such as mason jars, coffee filters, hot plates, pressure cookers, pillowcases, plastic tubing, gas cans, etc., to substitute for sophisticated laboratory equipment.

Another factor in the clandestine methamphetamine lab epidemic is the evolution of technology and the increased use of the Internet. While in the past, methamphetamine "chemists" closely guarded their "recipes"; today's age of modern computer technology has made "chemists" more willing to share their "recipes" of death. This form of information sharing allows wide dissemination of these techniques to anyone with computer access. Aside from marijuana, methamphetamine is the only widely abused illegal drug that is capable of being grown or readily manufactured by the abuser. A cocaine or heroin addict cannot produce cocaine or heroin, but a methamphetamine addict only has to turn on his computer to find a recipe identifying the chemicals and process required for production of the drug. Given the relative ease with which manufacturers are able to acquire precursor chemicals [chemicals used to manufacture methamphetamine], and the unsophisticated nature of the production process, it is not difficult to see why this highly addictive drug and potentially explosive clandestine laboratories continue to appear across America. . . .

Of the 21 DEA Field Divisions, 15 identify the principal methamphetamine transporters in their areas as Mexican distributors. Mexican criminal groups control most mid-level and retail methamphetamine distribution in the Pacific, Southwest, and West Central regions as well as much of the distribution in the Great Lakes and Southeast regions. Mexican mid-level distributors sometimes supply methamphetamine to outlaw mo-

THE HISTORY OF DRUGS

Methods of Ingesting Amphetamines

Early methods of ingesting amphetamines included taking the drug orally, sniffing it through the nose, and injecting it into the bloodstream.

The methods to ingest the amphetamine type drugs has had a developing metamorphosis. Originally the drug was taken orally (for prescription purposes it still is) or by sniffing it through the nose (insufflate) into the nasal passages, and by injections into the blood stream. Now there is a chronic problem of taking the drug. It is smoked, which accelerates its effects. After the smoke enters the lungs, it is immediately absorbed into the blood and quickly reaches the brain. This results in an almost instantaneous, more intense, intoxication referred to by users as being "fried."

Snorting and intravenous use create adverse effects to the user. Those who inject will frequently develop abscesses, ulcerations, and welts around the injection sites. Those who snort the drug must endure the terrible burning sensation while the drug goes in their nose and down their throat.

When the drug is smoked the dosage amount is small, even as little as one hundredth of a gram (0.01). The standard dosage for taking it orally or snorting the drug is traditionally between five hundredths (0.05) and one tenth (0.10) of a gram. These amounts greatly depend upon the tolerance of the user and the quality of the drug. Small level dealers will do what is referred to as "stepping on the drug" which is diluting the drug with cutting agents. Thus, the seller makes more money.

California Narcotic Officers' Association, *Narcotic Educational Foundation of America*, 2003, www.cnoa.org.

torcycle gangs and Hispanic gangs for retail distribution throughout the country. Caucasian independent distributors are active throughout the country, particularly in the Great Lakes, Mid-Atlantic, and Southeast regions and in the Midwestern states of Arkansas, Iowa, Kansas, and Missouri, where methamphetamine produced in small laboratories is distributed to a limited number of local customers. Outlaw motorcycle gangs distribute methamphetamine throughout the country, including the Great Lakes region and are principal distributors in the New England and New York/New Jersey regions. Asian methamphetamine distributors (Filipino, Japanese, Korean, Thai, and Vietnamese) are active in the Pacific region, although Mexican criminal groups trafficking in "ice" [a crystalline form of methamphetamine] have supplanted Asian criminal groups as the dominant distributors of this drug in Hawaii. . . .

Mexican Drug Traffic

For the first time in law enforcement history, beginning around 1994, Mexican drug trafficking organizations operating out of Mexico and California began to take control of the production and distribution of methamphetamine from outlaw motorcycle gangs. DEA estimates that the majority of the U.S. methamphetamine production and distribution is controlled by Mexican crime groups operating out of Mexico, California and the Southwestern United States. Outlaw motorcycle gangs remain active in methamphetamine production, but do not produce anywhere near the quantities now being distributed by the Mexican organizations. The dominant presence of these Mexican methamphetamine trafficking groups can be partially attributed to their access to chemicals and established distribution networks.

These groups have established contacts with chemical suppliers in Europe, Canada, Asia and the Far East, who provide access to precursor chemicals, reagents and solvents. The resulting availability of ton quantities of chemicals, such as ephedrine and pseudoephedrine, has permitted these groups to establish and operate large-scale clandestine laboratories in Mexico and California. These laboratories are capable of producing unprecedented quantities of methamphetamine, saturating the wholesale/retail markets throughout the United States. Many of the "super labs" (laboratories capable of producing 10 or more pounds of methamphetamine within a production cycle) seized in the United States have been associated with Mexican traffickers.

These trafficking groups are also often involved in the distribution of other illicit drugs such as marijuana, cocaine, and heroin. Through the distribution of these illicit substances, over the years these groups have established transportation and distribution networks throughout the United States. The exploitation of these existing distribution networks and the production capability of their clandestine laboratories has enabled the Mexican groups to establish national dominance in the manufacture and distribution of methamphetamine.

Four recent large seizures of pseudoephedrine illustrate Mexican traffickers' ability to obtain large quantities of precursor chemicals from international sources and to adapt to changes in the availability of Canadian pseudoephedrine. Between March 21, and April 25, 2003, in excess of 22 million pseudoephedrine tablets were seized in Panama and Laredo, Texas. The tablets were manufactured in Hong Kong and destined for Mexico.

Reporting on the exact number of methamphetamine clandestine laboratories seized in Mexico is inconsistent. Official Government of Mexico figures as reported in the International Narcotics Control Strategic Report (INCSR) reflect that 10 labs were destroyed in 2002, down from the 18 seized in 2001. In 2002, according to information provided by Mexican authorities in Baja California, however, 53 labs were seized in Baja alone and Mexico Interpol [crime control organization] reports that 13 labs were seized or destroyed. This discrepancy may reflect the limited resources and lack of coordination in Mexico to successfully attack the problem. In any case, the relatively small number of clandestine laboratories seized belies the large-scale production of methamphetamine that is believed to occur in Mexico.

The Spread of Small Toxic Labs

On a much smaller production and distribution scale are the independent operators of small toxic labs (STLs), which collectively account for approximately 95 percent of the clandestine laboratories seized in the United States. These STLs produce ounce quantities of methamphetamine for local use and distribution while generating significant quantities of hazardous waste during each production cycle. Small, rural communities are now recognizing the fiscal, environmental, health, and safety issues that are associated with the operation of these independent laboratories.

STLs initially emerged as a problem in the Midwest in the early to mid-1990s. After the introduction of methamphetamine to this area by Mexican trafficking organizations, users discovered that they could produce their own methamphetamine. These operations became extremely popular because of the simplicity of the Birch method (commonly known as the "Nazi" method) and pseudoephedrine/iodine/red phosphorus methods of manufacturing methamphetamine. Each of these methods relies on readily available and inexpensive products and an uncomplicated production process to manufacture methamphetamine. The ease of manufacturing and availability of chemicals contributed greatly to the dramatic growth and spread of these labs throughout the United States. Anhydrous ammonia, while not readily available at the retail level, is extensively used in rural areas. Anhydrous ammonia can be easily stolen from nurse tanks stored on farms or at farming cooperatives, train tanker cars that transport the chemical, or from one of the anhydrous pipelines.

The size of the lab does not matter when it comes to the

danger level involved. In fact, the STLs are often more dangerous than the larger operations. The "cooks" are generally less
experienced and have little regard for the consequences arising from the use of toxic, explosive, and poisonous chemicals.
EPIC [El Paso Intelligence Center] reported that during 2002,
there were 126 explosions and 208 fires as the result of clandestine laboratories. The threats posed by clandestine laboratories are not limited to fire, explosions, poisonous gas, drug
abuse and booby traps; the chemical contamination caused by
the hazardous waste also endangers the nation's environment.

The combination of demand, ease of production, and a rural
setting has led to the explosion of STLs that now plague the
Midwestern and Southern States, and has continued eastward
to New York. Despite the fact that the majority of these labs
produce relatively small amounts of methamphetamine, their
proliferation has imposed terrific burdens on law enforcement
and other agencies in states such as Missouri. In 1992, Missouri reported only two clandestine laboratory seizures; in
2002, 1,046 labs were seized in that state. When dumpsites
and other seizures (chemicals, glassware and equipment) are
included, this total climbs to 2,747.

Enforcement Initiatives

DEA's efforts to address methamphetamine production and distribution incorporate the assets of the Offices of Domestic and
International Operations, Diversion, Intelligence, Forensic Sciences, and Training. DEA focuses assets on both domestic
groups, which represent the largest number of methamphetamine laboratories seized in the United States, and international
organizations, particularly Mexican groups which produce the
majority of methamphetamine trafficked in the U.S. The following are key components of DEA's methamphetamine initiative:

1. Elimination of Small Toxic Labs

Working arm-in-arm with state and local law enforcement
counterparts, DEA eliminates STL operators that impact com-

munities throughout the United States. In addition to providing investigative support to state and local agencies, DEA assists state and local authorities with hazardous waste removal, prevention, public awareness, training, and legislative programs that are associated with methamphetamine. DEA cases involving methamphetamine have almost tripled from 1,171 in 1995 to over 3,000 in 2002.

2. Chemical Control

DEA uses the precursor control program to identify and target the most significant sources of methamphetamine precursor chemicals. DEA works domestically with legitimate handlers of precursor chemicals to ensure that these chemicals are not diverted for illicit use.

3. Priority Targeting Program

One of DEA's most aggressive enforcement efforts to attack these organizations is the utilization of the Priority Targeting Program. Once identified and designated as priority targets, these investigations are provided with substantial financial and manpower resources. Since the inception of the Priority Targeting Program in 2000, DEA has dismantled or disrupted over 60 priority target methamphetamine trafficking organizations. . . .

Operation Stopgap

Operation Stopgap was a cooperative effort directed by DEA's Nashville Resident Office in conjunction with local law enforcement, which identified, targeted, and federally prosecuted small independent laboratory operators in a six county area known as the Cumberland Plateau. This OCDETF [Organized Crime Drug Enforcement Task Force] case culminated during October 2001, with the arrests of over 175 individuals and the seizure of approximately 150 methamphetamine laboratories.

In April 2003, 18 individuals were arrested in New Mexico and California, in connection with a Mexican methamphetamine and crack cocaine distribution organization. As part of this continuing investigation, in June, DEA's Albuquerque District Office and state and local agencies arrested 12 additional individuals on federal charges and 38 on State of New Mexico charges. This organization was responsible for the distribution of 60 pounds of methamphetamine on a monthly basis. Over $291,000 in assets were seized in addition to 12 vehicles, 24 firearms (including 4 assault-type weapons), and 21 pounds of methamphetamine.

In May 2003, the U.S. District Court for the Western District of Oklahoma sentenced Norma El-Samad to 97 months incarceration on drug and money laundering charges. El-Samad owned Norma's Enterprises of Oklahoma City, which purchased over 14 million 60mg. pseudoephedrine tablets from Summa Laboratories in Mineral Wells, Texas. DEA was able to provide convincing evidence that most, if not all, of the pseudoephedrine was directed toward clandestine methamphetamine laboratory operations.

In August of 2002, DEA working with the Riverside (California) County Sheriff's Department and the Riverside Police Department, arrested over 57 individuals in connection with a two-year investigation targeting a Mexican trafficking organization, which was involved in the manufacture and distribution of methamphetamine. Investigators seized in excess of 33 pounds of methamphetamine, 196 gallons of methamphetamine in solution, 8 pounds of "ice", 80 exotic vehicles and over $500,000 in cash. . . .

Methamphetamine Laboratories and Children

In addition to the evident toll on law enforcement resources, the demands on medical, social, environmental, and public heath and safety services continue to grow. This is particularly true when it comes to the health and safety of children exposed to the ravages of this illegal substance. STLs account for the vast majority of clandestine labs seized and are often discovered in vehicles, buildings, and homes. Many of these lab sites are also locations where children live and play. In 2002, over 2,000 children were present during the seizure of clandestine laboratories nationwide. Twenty-two of those children encountered were reported injured and two were killed.

More than any other controlled substance, methamphetamine trafficking endangers children through exposure to drug use/abuse, neglect, physical and sexual abuse, toxic chemicals, hazardous waste, fire, and explosion. In response to these tragic phenomena, DEA has enhanced its Victim Witness Program to identify, inform, refer, and report these incidents to the proper state agencies. Each of DEA's Field Divisions has a Victim/Witness Coordinator to ensure that all endangered children are reported. DEA prepares an annual report for the Attorney General regarding this matter. This DEA program guarantees that endangered children are identified and that the child's immediate safety is addressed at the scene through coordination with child welfare and health care service providers.

DEA also works with various state and local Drug Endangered Children (DEC) programs. DEC programs protect endangered children through the formation of multidisciplinary teams, which consist of child protective services, medical and public health professionals, environmental, and law enforcement personnel. DEC ensures that child endangerment cases are developed along with the clandestine laboratory investigation. DEA encourages regional U.S. Attorney's, when applicable, to utilize the enhanced sentencing guidelines promulgated as directed in the "Children's Health Act of 2000". This legislation mandates severe penalties for methamphetamine manufacturers whose operations pose a threat to minors. . . .

DEA is combating the methamphetamine epidemic currently being experienced by the United States on several fronts. DEA is targeting Mexican trafficking organizations, who control the majority of the methamphetamine produced and distributed in this country. Additionally, DEA is working closely with state and local law enforcement to eliminate the spread of small toxic labs. DEA's efforts also include preventing diversion and targeting the traffickers of precursor chemicals on a domestic and international level, as well as providing training and assistance to state and local law enforcement officers throughout the United States.

As a single mission agency, DEA will continue to devote its resources to identify, investigate and dismantle the organizations responsible for the spread of methamphetamine across our country.

Methamphetamine Is Rural America's Number One Threat

Paul Solotaroff

In rural northwest America, crystal methamphetamine abuse is rampant. In this selection, journalist Paul Solotaroff relates the details of his shocking visit to Granite Falls, a former logging town north of Seattle, Washington, where children are becoming junkies. Cheap, easy to make, and sometimes instantly addictive, crystal methamphetamine causes irreversible brain damage. Only about 6 percent of "meth freaks" are able to kick the habit. In Granite Falls, the crime rate has shot up drastically and the majority of violent criminals are involved with methamphetamines in some way. From small towns like this, meth is migrating to cities across America. Paul Solotaroff is a former editor at the *Village Voice*, an alternative newsweekly, and a journalist whose work has twice been nominated for the Pulitzer Prize. Solotaroff has written for a number of national magazines, including *Esquire, GQ, Vogue,* and *Rolling Stone.*

It looks less like a crime scene and still less like a farm—than it does a tour of an unhinged mind. Out behind the barn on this half-mile-square spread at the base of the Cascade Mountains in Washington state, there is a riot of stolen cars and trucks, parts stripped and chassis mangled. A months-old Lexus, its seats splayed beside it, lies nose-down in mud. Two white Chevy sport-utes, their axles spavined, hunker on bales of hay.

Paul Solotaroff, "Plague in the Heartland," *Rolling Stone*, January 23, 2003, p. 48.

Lawn mowers and dirt bikes sprawl, tires up, in poses of mechanized porn. Thirty yards away, in a vast stockade, mill twenty of the skinniest cows in the county. There were eighty head out there as late as [just a month ago], then the bank came up and seized sixty of the herd to satisfy unpaid debts.

"That's what happens when you start smoking meth—people repossess your cows," says Chuck Allen, chief of the Granite Falls police force and one of the dozen or so cops and Snohomish County deputies buzzing around the grounds. In the five years since methamphetamine entrenched itself in this former logging town north of Seattle, Allen's work life has consisted of responding to one outrage after another, each more numbing than the last. The month before, there were the tweakers (as meth users are known) who clubbed to death seventeen newborn calves. Before that, it was the boy, high out of his mind, who fancied his thick skull bulletproof and blew much of it off with a .25. Like no drug before it—not crack, coke, Ecstasy or smack—meth has so swamped this rural community that it has largely come to define it. Granite Falls, a town of 2,600, is now notorious as Methville or Cranktown among the hundreds of kids bused to school here. That is unkind, and in any case unjust: There isn't a town from Tacoma to the Canadian border that couldn't as easily have earned that mantle. Meth—cheap, potent and insuperably addictive—is everywhere in the Pacific Northwest, and coming soon to a town near you.

Allen, a stout man with Elvis sideburns and a thatch of ginger hair, walks me around to the barn. The squalor inside rivals the scene outdoors, a tumult of garbage and cow shit. Additionally, there's a piercing stench that scours the back of my throat. On a bench near the door is an array of buckets rigged to a kerosene vat. This, says Allen, is where the thirty-two-year-old farmer "cooked," then dried, his meth.

"Battery acid, ammonia, paint thinner, lye that's what you're smelling," says Allen. "Take a bunch of the most toxic solvents there are, mix 'em up with some Sudafed pills and put that in your pipe and smoke it. Your teeth'll fall out, your skin'll scab off, and a month from now you'll be coughing up chunks of your lung—but hey, what the hell? Party on, right?"

That isn't so much bitterness as bafflement talking. Despite dozens of local deaths attributed to meth, and a pitched campaign by school officials to scare teens off the drug, it remains wildly popular on the party scene, which starts as young as fifth grade.

"These aren't no-tooth yokels from trailer parks," says Allen. "They're kids whose moms and dads work at Boeing.". . .

Meth Is a New Kind of Danger

When we speak of the drug plagues of the last half-century—heroin, the last half—the postwar Harlem; crack the deathblow to countless downtowns—what comes to mind first is the chaos they've wrought, the derangement of public and private life. But for all the pain and confusion sown, drug epidemics were actually orderly things, obeying their own deep logic. Invariably—until now—they began offshore, imported to America from exotic locales such as Bolivia and Southeast Asia. Invariably—until now—they took root in port towns, opening markets in New York or Miami before hopscotching west to other cities. Invariably—until now—they then radiated outward, moving from megalopolises to suburban towns, and from there to the exurbs and farmlands. And invariably—until now—they hit the poor hardest, entrenching themselves like rogue bacteria in the playgrounds and stairwells of projects. . . .

Now those rules are void; meth has rewritten the book. As the first epidemic born on our soil, it is seeding the ground for future plagues while confounding cops and drug czars. It is made, for instance, from legal and easily obtained ingredients, not from opiates that must be smuggled ashore. It flows inward rather than outward, beginning in small towns before migrating to urban centers. (Having overwhelmed much of the rural Northwest, it's now one of the fastest-growing drugs in seven Western cities, among them Seattle, Denver and Salt

Lake City, and rivals crack use in Los Angeles and San Francisco.) And where other drugs targeted the inner cities, meth for the most part hits the middle class.

"Around here, crack and heroin have a ghetto stigma that doesn't apply to meth," says Rick Bart, the personable sheriff of Snohomish County, who, as the region's top cop, presides over a beleaguered staff of 230 deputies. "The kids here think it's a rave drug like Ecstasy, or just some cool thing they read about on the Internet. You can go online right now and find 300 Web sites with recipes on how to make it, then go out to the drugstore and home-supplies shop and pick up all the fixings. How in the world am I supposed to stop that—post a man in the allergy aisle at Walgreen's?"

Actually, that won't be necessary. Walk into a drugstore in Washington state and you'll find the Sudafed and Drixoral behind thick glass, padlocked like vintage scotch; taped to the sales case is a yellow sign limiting shoppers to two packs a day. This is the result of one of several new state laws aimed at keeping meth ingredients out of the hands of cooks. Ephedrine, found in most non-prescription cold drugs, is the key constituent of meth. State officials have also put restrictions on the sale of compounds such as anhydrous ammonia, a compressed liquid gas that cooks use to distill ephedrine during the volatile cooking process. (Get a drop of the stuff on you and it will burn through the skin, singeing right down to the bone.) Two years ago, anyone with a tank and the right tubing could buy as much chemical as he or she liked; now, it can be sold only to certified licensees, and in amounts of at least 500 gallons. That hasn't stopped thieves from raiding the plants or siphoning it into gas cans from rail cars. Recently, someone botched a heist at a local factory and released a cloud of ammonia that covered forty acres, forcing an entire town to evacuate.

"Understand that we're not dealing with the brightest bulbs; methheads either start dumb or get there fast," says Lynn Eul, the youth-violence and drug-prevention coordinator for the Snohomish County prosecutor's office. "The solvents used to make it literally gouge out their brain. After only a couple of weeks, tweakers suffer permanent brain damage. And that's not counting the neurochemical part. Meth addicts can't make dopamine anymore, which sends them into such a deep depression, they want to kill themselves or the people around them.". . .

Social Effects of Meth

Since 1998, when meth use reached plague levels in Snohomish County, every index of social misery has soared. The crime rate is up forty percent at a time when it fell sharply across the country. Jim Krider, the former county prosecutor, estimates that two-thirds of the violent criminals he tries use meth, cook it or sell it. The prison near his office, built for 300, sleeps 500 inmates on an average night, most doubled and tripled up in cells. The drumbeat goes on: Fostercare placements are up by a third, while admissions to the state's drug programs have jumped tenfold. "I could hit you over the head with lots more numbers—what's happened with ER admissions in the last years; the skyrocketing increase in domestic violence—but let's just put it like this: There isn't a single aspect of life in this state that hasn't been drastically hit by this drug," says Jim Chromey, the commander of Strategic Weapons and Tactics for the Washington State Patrol. "A whole generation is being lost out here, and we'll never get that back."

Like most deliriants, meth started out as something very different. Its first appearance in the medical literature, in 1887, was as a Victorian cure for narcolepsy [a sleep disorder]. Fifty years later, a tableted version showed promise as a bronchial aid and was prescribed by doctors in the U.S. and abroad despite evidence that it was psychoactive. Then, as now, its core element was ephedrine, which, taken in high doses, revved the nervous system with a sharp, swift burst of adrenaline. Such, in fact, was its stimulatory kick that by World War II, it was widely dispensed to both Allied and Axis troops, with the dispiriting result that many came home with ravening addictions. Thereafter, meth went underground, surfacing occasionally as powdered "crank" with outlaw-biker drugs, or as an injectable fluid spiking the pre-AIDS frenzy in gay clubs across the country. (During the first phase of use, meth is as potent an aphrodisiac as any; within months or even weeks, though, the brain's taste for pleasure is more or less permanently shorted, leaving the user incapable of arousal.)

Finally, in the Eighties, the big bang: A smokable version appeared. "I was running a clinic in Haight-Ashbury [a neighborhood in San Francisco] '88 when ice showed up on the street," says Dr. Alex Stalcup, a national authority on meth and a pioneer in the treatment of its addiction. "It was so powerful that you had a rush like nothing before it. In terms of dopamine triggered, it was the chemical equivalent of ten orgasms at once—and you didn't need a needle to get it. Once a drug bypasses the needle stage and induces a giant rush, you have the twin preconditions for an epidemic, which is exactly what we got here. Add to that the fact that it can be made at home, and we've gone from epidemic to pandemic, meaning it's so easily and widely available that you can't stop it."

Stalcup, who runs a premier treatment center near San Francisco, has been in the trenches of the drug wars for most of four decades and says he's never seen anything as pernicious as meth. "Forget, for a moment, what it does to kids while they're in the binge-tweak cycle—the rage and delusions, the spontaneous violence. The true hell starts when they try to get sober and find that meth has stripped out their higher functioning, much of which won't come back. They can't process words, can't think abstractly, can't, in fact, remember what they did five minutes ago. Worse, their psychic skin has been peeled away and they're indescribably raw. As we speak, there's a twelve-year-old girl down the hall, curled up on the floor, screaming, 'I can't take it, I can't take it.'". . .

Dr. Alice Huber, a researcher at the University of Washington and a frontline player in two landmark meth studies, says that the pain and despair in the first phase of rehab make it all but unbearable to continue: "The biggest hurdle to treatment is keeping them there. They're in agony and we can't quell it. As a rule, you have to wait at least six months before they can begin to understand what's being said to them. But with managed care, you're lucky to get two weeks."

Meth Is Spreading Like a Tidal Wave

Given that kind of odds, it would certainly behoove local and federal authorities to prevent the drug's spread to other regions. But there, too, the news is disheartening. Meth, which began its run in central California and took I-5 north to Oregon and Washington, has already traveled the eastwest corridors to the heartland and Southern states. Drug gangs operating along I-80 have flooded the Corn Belt with crystal ice, the most potent form of the drug. (There are three different grades of meth being sold: Crank, a foul-smelling yellow powder, is generally snorted, not smoked; lith, short for the lithium culled from batteries to distill out chemical harshness, is a smokable paste that induces a fierce rush and costs about twice what crank does; and ice, triple-crystallized of all impurities to create an unmatched high, sells for $150 a gram and is almost instantly addictive.) Nebraska and Indiana are glutted with meth, and Missouri has recently supplanted California as the number-one state for labs seized. Down south, I-40 has become a superconductor for sales to rural whites. Both of the Carolinas report full-on plagues, while in Tennessee home cooks are so pervasive that child-abuse charges are being added to drug counts if a minor is found on the premises.

"Meth is the number-one threat to rural America," says Will Glasby, the chief of media relations for the Drug Enforcement Agency. "If you look at a map, it's like a tidal wave moving east from California and the Northwest states. Last year, we took down 7,000 labs, many in the middle of the country.

Some were in areas that had never seen crime before, let alone drug gangs and shootouts. We're hopeful it won't reach Eastern cities. Because if it ever does land in urban America. . . ." Glasby stops a moment to choose his words. "Well, let's just say there'll be major problems."

Pressed on what the DEA [Drug Enforcement Administration] is doing specifically to stem the flow of meth, Glasby cites its long-standing work with local cops as well as a series of town-hall meetings that were attended last summer [2002] by the agency's head, Asa Hutchinson. Told that this seems a faint response to the "number one threat" in the country, Glasby makes mention of harsh budget constraints, saying the agency has "many priorities and limited dollars." Curiously, one priority that's well-funded, however, is the DEA's war on medical marijuana, featuring armed invasions of hospice co-ops in California and elsewhere. If the agency can summon the resources to roust terminally ill seniors and cuff them at gunpoint to their walkers, couldn't it find the money and additional manpower to intervene on behalf of kids? . . .

One Town Faces Meth

When a town is confronted by a social ill, it usually conducts itself in one of two ways. Paralyzed by shame, it denies the problem until the moment to effectively act is lost, or it comes together with candor and grace to meet the crisis head-on. After a timid start, Granite Falls did the latter, shucking its down-home modesty to admit it was swamped by drugs. A coalition of businessmen and school officials formed to draft a plan of attack, which included a youth meth summit that drew a thousand kids from the area last summer [2002]. Congregants from churches went door-to-door, passing out packets about the epidemic in progress to parents of school kids. And the police force joined cops from neighboring towns to take down street-level dealers and buyers, assembling an informal SWAT team. Although the yield of these efforts is hard to gauge, the pas-

sion that informed them is front and center: This town is ter-
rified of losing its children.

"I do have other duties, but this seems like all I deal with:
another kid tweaking out in class," says Bridgette Perrigoue,
the psychologist at Granite Falls High School. "They come in
dirty, not having eaten or slept, and sit there clawing at the
skin on their arms 'cause they think there's bugs underneath
it. Or they threaten the kids next to them and scream at the
teacher, then disappear for a week. And mind you, these are
eighth- and ninth-graders."

I had spent much of the morning with three such kids in a
conference room down the hall. Only months removed from
the treatment programs that, for the moment at least, broke
their falls, the three, who happened to be bright, verbal girls,
described life in the thresher of meth. Heather, whose friends
turned her on at twelve and who was soon robbing houses to
support her habit, plowed a car into a tree at eighty miles an
hour and spent a year learning to walk again. Kale, who
waited till thirteen to start, ran away to sleep on drug dealers'
floors and went missing, on and off, for two years; her pretty
face is fretted, still, with contrail scars from gouging it during
all-night tweaks. And Neva, 16, snorted a line three years ago
and soon found herself on the streets of Everett, a rough-and-
tumble city fifteen miles south. Running with a posse of older
boys, she was stealing and dealing and on the verge of being
pimped out for faster money when the cops took her in for loi-
tering. After two stints in rehab, which she describes as "tor-
ture" months of round-the-clock drug sweats and break-
downs—she is back in school and determined to shine, though
her old friends keep calling at night.

Meth's Behind Every Rock and Cranny

"That's the thing about this town—there's no escaping it;
meth's behind every rock and cranny," she says. "Go to the
skate park, it's there; go to Burger King, it's there; about the

only thing you can do is run home. And I'm getting along better with my mom and all, but it sucks that I, you know, have to hide out. I mean, what am I supposed to do for the next three years? Just 'cause I'm sober doesn't mean I'm a nun."

Neva has been clean now for nine and a half months. I ask if she still gets cravings.

"Yeah, sometimes," she murmurs, casting a furtive glance at the two girls across the table. "Like, I taste it, still, in the back of my throat. You never forget that taste."

"Me either," says Heather. "It's just super-intense, the most amped-up high you've ever had. You think you can do anything, like fly a plane or beat up dudes. I used to get real violent when I tweaked."

"But that's not why you do it—at least why I did," Kale intercuts. "It's more of, your friends are all using, and you want to be with them, so you go ahead and smoke too. And at first I didn't like it. I mean, yeah, it was all this energy and stuff—I was having the most amazing thoughts. But later on that night, you know, the fear kicked in and I was totally bugged out and wired. I remember running to the park and hiding behind bushes because I thought everyone was a spy for my mom. Finally, I got so freaked I was gonna die right there that I walked to the police station and said, 'Arrest me,' and wound up in jail for a while.". . .

"And that wasn't enough to scare you off?"

"Well, for a minute, it was. I was in detention a month—they do that when you run away here. But then I got out again and saw my friends and—well, that's the problem with meth-heads. They're persistent."

The Threat of Ecstasy

Lynn M. Smith and Asa Hutchinson

The first part of this selection is testimony given by a young woman who became addicted to Ecstasy, a drug chemically related to amphetamines. Although she was a straight-A student who never expected to become involved in drugs, the young woman was captivated by the intense high she felt the first time she took Ecstasy. As she increasingly used the drug, however, her horrible experiences caused her to be hospitalized and eventually motivated her to become a spokesperson against Ecstasy.

The second part of this selection addresses the threat of Ecstasy to the youth of America. In 2001, emergency rooms were visited by 5,542 Ecstasy users, a dramatic rise over previous years. Studies also indicate that recreational users can develop permanent brain damage. The Drug Enforcement Administration is working to raise awareness about the drug as well as pursue domestic and international Ecstasy trafficking organizations. Lynn M. Smith is a spokesperson for the Partnership for a Drug-Free America and the anti-Ecstasy movement. Asa Hutchinson is the undersecretary for border and transportation security and former administrator of the Drug Enforcement Administration.

I hear a lot of people talking about Ecstasy, calling it a fun, harmless drug. All I can think is, "if they only knew." I grew up in a small, rural town in Pennsylvania. It's one of those places where everyone knows your name, what you did, what you ate and so on. They certainly knew me—I was a straight-A stu-

Lynn M. Smith and Asa Hutchinson, testimony and statement before the House Committee on Government Reform, Subcommittee on Criminal Justice, Drug Policy, and Human Resources, Washington, DC, September 19, 2002.

dent involved in many school activities. I was one of the popular kids, liked by all the different crowds, involved in home-
coming, regularly cast in school theater productions. Drugs
never played a part in my life. They were never a question—I
was too involved and focused on other things. I always
dreamed of moving to New York City to study acting and pursue a career in theater. My dream came true when my mom
brought me to the city to attend acting school. As you can
imagine, it was quite a change from home, I was exposed to
new people, new ideas and a completely new way of life—a
way of life that exposed me to drugs. Most of the people that
I met and spent time with in acting school had already been
doing drugs for years. I guess I felt that by using drugs, I would
become a part of their world and it would deepen my friend-
ships with them to new levels. I tried pot, even a little cocaine,
but it was Ecstasy that changed my life forever. I remember the
feeling I had the first time I did Ecstasy: complete and utter
bliss. I could feel the pulse of the universe; I let every breath,
touch and molecule move my soul. It was as if I had unlocked
some sort of secret world; it was as if I'd found heaven. And I
have to admit, I wondered how anything that made you feel so
good could possibly be bad.

At first, going to school and holding down two jobs to stay
afloat left little time for partying, but as time went by things
changed. I graduated, had a steady job, made more new
friends—and began to use drugs, especially Ecstasy, more frequently. As I did, I actually started to look down on those who
did not. I surrounded myself only with those who did. Looking
back on my old friends, I see how we were all so similar, not
just in our drug use but in a deeper sense. We were all broken
in some way, feeling sad, hurt and alone. Whether it was from
a difficult childhood, a broken heart, or feelings of insecurity.
We were a crowd of lost souls wanting so badly to be a part of
something. I had gone from a girl who never used drugs to a
woman who couldn't imagine life without them. Fortunately—
at least as I saw it—all my friends did Ecstasy, and since my

boyfriend sold it, I rarely paid for anything. My weekends were spent popping pills and dancing at one of the many clubs In New York City—but it didn't really matter where I was. Clubs, bars, apartments—anywhere, anytime became a good place and a good time to use. My weekends began on Thursday and ran until Sunday.

I had come to New York dreaming of a career in the theater. Drugs didn't rob me of that dream, but they did make me willing to forget about it. It wasn't that I stopped getting parts because I was using; I just stopped auditioning. Sometimes I stopped eating and sleeping. I worked only two days a week to support my habit. The rest of the time was spent getting high, almost always on Ecstasy. The utter bliss of my first Ecstasy experience was a distant memory. Of course, I never could recapture that first high, no matter how much Ecstasy I took.

Sinking into a Dark, Lonely Place

In five months, I went from living somewhat responsibly while pursuing my dream to a person who didn't care about a thing— and the higher I got, the deeper I sank into a dark, lonely place. When I did sleep, I had nightmares and the shakes. I had pasty skin, a throbbing head and the beginnings of paranoia, but I ignored it all, thinking it was normal. Until the night I thought I was dying. On this night, I was sitting on the couch with my boyfriend and roommates, watching a movie and feeling normal when suddenly, I felt as if I needed to jump out of my skin. Racing thoughts, horrible images and hallucinations crept through my mind. I thought I was seeing the devil, and I repeatedly asked my friends if I was dead. I was pacing frantically back and forth, incapable of relaxing or understanding anything that was going on around me. On top of all this, I felt as if I was having a heart attack. The worst thing was those moments when I could see myself, and what I had become. Somehow, I managed to pick up the phone and call my mom in the middle of the night, telling her to come get me. She did, pulling me out of my apartment at the next morning.

I didn't know who I was or where I was as my mom drove me back to my family's hospital in Pennsylvania. I spent most of the drive curled up in the back seat while my younger sister tried to keep me calm. I think she and my mom were afraid I'd jump out of the moving car at any moment—and given my state of mind at the time, I can't say I blame them. When we finally got to the hospital, I was committed to the psychiatric ward. I spent the next 14 days there in a state of extreme confusion. This is what Ecstasy gave me—but it didn't stop there.

While I was in the hospital, my doctors performed something called a neuro-spec scan of my brain. I couldn't believe my eyes when I saw the results. The scan showed several dark splotches on the image of my brain, and my doctors told me those were areas—areas that carry out memory functions— where the activity of my brain had been changed in some way. Because I used other drugs, the doctors could not say that my heavy Ecstasy abuse was solely responsible for this. But this much I know for sure: There's nothing in my medical history that could have contributed to this.

Going Public with the Story

Since I saw that scan 2 years ago, my life has forever been change. I have dedicated myself to educating America's youth about the perils of Ecstasy abuse. I went public with my story in hopes of preventing others from making the same mistakes. I have become a spokesperson for the Partnership for a Drug Free America and the anti-Ecstasy movement. I have appeared on the Oprah Winfrey Show, MTV's True Life, the Ananda Lewis Show, and have been interviewed by dozens of reporters. I am actively speaking at schools and universities around the country to talk about my story and the need for drug education and awareness. My participation in a news conference regarding the launch of the first national education campaign targeting Ecstasy was a critical element in the event's success,

helping it to garner coverage from nearly 700 broadcast outlets nationwide. My story is powerful, and my commitment to
using my experience to help others is considerable.

I have been given a second chance, and that's not something that everyone gets.

Ecstasy (MDMA) Overview

MDMA, [3,4-methylinedioxymethamphetamine, commonly referred to as Ecstasy] a Schedule I [see "How Drugs Are Classified" in Appendix] drug, is the most widely abused club drug
in America. MDMA users experience both hallucinogenic and
stimulant effects which last several hours. Accounts from users
describe the drug as intensifying their senses, particularly the
external sense of touch and an inward feeling of "closeness" or
"empathy." They will often dance with fluorescent light sticks,
use Vicks Vapor Rub and other miscellaneous items to increase stimulation and enhance the drug's effects.

Abusing MDMA can produce a number of adverse effects
including severe dehydration, exhaustion, nausea, hallucinations, chills, sweating, increase in body temperature, tremors,
involuntary teeth clenching, muscle cramping, and blurred vi-
sion. MDMA may also create after-effects such as anxiety,
paranoia, and depression. Recent MDMA related deaths were
associated with core body temperatures of 107 to 109 degrees.

In 1998 a study conducted by researchers at Johns Hopkins
Medical Center and funded by the National Institute of Mental
Health revealed that habitual MDMA abusers suffer long-term
neurological damage. The study indicates that recreational
MDMA users may be in danger of developing permanent brain
damage that might manifest itself in the form of depression,
anxiety, memory loss, or neuro-psychiatric disorder.

In addition, there have been numerous major scientific
studies published in peer reviewed journals which have shown
significant impairments in memory and learning in individuals
who have ingested MDMA. Combined with the knowledge that

all of these drugs are clandestinely produced in unsanitary laboratories which result in uncontrolled purity, the threat to public health and safety is immense. . . .

MDMA Traffickers

MDMA is synthetically manufactured in clandestine laboratories predominately in Western Europe in the Netherlands and Belgium, which produce the vast majority of the MDMA consumed worldwide. A typical clandestine laboratory is capable of producing 20–30 kilograms of MDMA per day, with one kilogram of MDMA producing approximately 7,000 tablets. Dutch Police reported the seizure of one laboratory capable of producing approximately 100 kilograms of MDMA per day.

Most often, MDMA consumed in the United States is manufactured by Dutch chemists, and transported or distributed by various factions of Israeli and Russian Organized Crime groups. These groups recruit and utilize American, Israeli and western European nationals as couriers. Couriers can smuggle 2 to 5 kilograms on their person, and 10 kilograms of MDMA in specially designed luggage. In addition to the use of couriers, these organizations commonly exploit commercial mail services to arrange delivery of their merchandise.

The drug trafficking organizations involved in MDMA distribution are brought together by the enormous profit realized in these ventures. Although estimates vary, the cost of producing one MDMA tablet is between $.50–$1.00. The wholesale price for MDMA tablets range from $1.00–$2.00, contingent on the volume purchased. Once the MDMA reaches the United States, a domestic cell distributor will charge from $6 to $12 per tablet. The MDMA retailer, in turn, will distribute the MDMA for $20 to $30 per tablet.

MDMA traffickers utilize major airports in Europe as transshipment points for MDMA destined to the United States. Los Angeles, New York, and Miami are currently the major "gateway cities" for the influx of MDMA. These three cities reflect the greatest number of arrests and seizure of MDMA within our borders. The largest MDMA seizure in the United States occurred in Los Angeles, California, where DEA and U.S. Customs seized over 700 pounds. Because of increased law enforcement awareness, Israeli traffickers are adjusting their routes and modes of transportation in order to circumvent detection and interdiction by law enforcement officials. These adjustments include a shift in transportation routes from these three "gateway cities" to other ports of entry in the United States.

Although Israeli and Russian MDMA trafficking organizations dominate the MDMA market in the United States, other drug trafficking organizations based in Colombia, the Dominican Republic, Asia, and Mexico have entered MDMA trade. As Ecstasy proves more profitable and as law enforcement pressures force the traffickers to re-group, the U.S. MDMA trade will become increasingly diverse.

Europe will most likely remain the primary source region for MDMA, at least, in the near term. Dominican and/or Colombian nationals smuggling cocaine to Europe have exchanged their cocaine for MDMA pills, a significant quantity of which will be destined for U.S. cities. However, it appears, at least for now, that MDMA production is securely entrenched in Europe.

MDMA production also appears to be gaining a foothold in Asia and Australia. Indonesia authorities recently seized a large-scale MDMA laboratory in Jakarta and over 300 pounds of MDMA. Given the ready availability of precursor chemicals in Asia, it is possible that Asian production of MDMA will increase in the future.

Raves: "Dancing in Darkness"

Club drugs have become an integral part of the rave scene. Raves gained popularity in Europe in the 1980s and appeared in the United States during the late 1980s and early 1990s. Raves are all night dance parties driven by synthesized "techno", "industrial" or other forms of pulsating music. Named "Drug Taking Festivals" by police, raves are typically held in warehouses, clubs, fields, or any other location that can accommodate a large number of people. The open distribution of MDMA and other club drugs has become commonplace at many of these venues.

Raves are organized, promoted, and financed by local and national enterprises that advertise through word of mouth, fliers, posters, telephone, radio, and the Internet. In fact, many raves are advertised as "drug and alcohol-free" in order to give partygoers and parents a false sense of security. Typically, ravers are between 12 and 25 years old, come from middle to upper-middle class economic backgrounds and from a wide variety of ethnic and national identities. . . .

Initiatives Against Rave Promoters

The State Palace Theater Investigation, which was conducted by the DEA [Drug Enforcement Administration] New Orleans Division in conjunction with the New Orleans Police Department and the U.S. Attorney's Office in New Orleans, serves as an excellent model of the resourcefulness of law enforcement in addressing the threat of club drugs.

During the course of this investigation, DEA agents learned that, over the past two years, 400 to 500 teenagers and young adults had been treated at local emergency rooms for overdose related illnesses, following their attendance at rave events hosted by the State Palace Theater.

As a result of the investigation, the company, in a plea agreement, agreed to pay a $100,000 fine. Perhaps most significant is the fact that, since the completion of the operation, club drug related overdoses in New Orleans have dropped 90%, with Ecstasy overdoses disappearing altogether. This statistic clearly shows a very strong correlation between rave activity and club drug overdoses resulting in emergency room visits. . . .

DEA began to focus national attention on the MDMA and club drugs in 2000, when the agency hosted the *International*

Conference on Ecstasy and Club Drugs in partnership with approximately 300 officials from domestic and foreign law enforcement, judicial, chemical, prevention and treatment communities. During the conference, several demand reduction objectives
were developed which have been institutionalized by DEA.
These objectives include:

- Providing accurate, complete, and current information on
  the scientific findings and medical effects of club drugs
  on the human body;
- Working with local, state, and other federal agencies and
  nonprofit organizations in an effort to advance drug education and prevention;
- Enhancing parental knowledge of raves and club drugs
  and engage their active participation in education and
  prevention of drug abuse;
- Educating high school and college students on the reali-
  ties of raves and the effects of club drugs on the human
  body.

In addition, DEA recently hosted a series of *Regional Club
Drug Conferences* in local communities as a way to develop effective enforcement and prevention strategies by bringing together federal, state, and local experts already familiar with
the club drug issue. Similar regional conferences were also
held in Chicago, Illinois, and San Diego, California. . . .

Club drug trafficking and abuse and the associated horrific
effects that accompany the abuse and distribution of these
drugs continue to be a priority for the Drug Enforcement Administration. DEA will continue to work with legislators, educators, prevention specialists, community action groups, and
law enforcement to raise awareness and educate America's
youth about the dangers of club drugs and all illegal drugs. In
addition, DEA will pursue domestic and international MDMA
and other club trafficking organizations to protect America's
borders from the horrors of these debilitating drugs.

Methamphetamine Abuse Is an AIDS Risk Factor

AIDS Alert

When the AIDS epidemic began in the late 1970s in the United States, researchers did not recognize its connection with meth-amphetamine drug abuse. According to one AIDS researcher, however, many people's histories of meth drug abuse were among the earliest AIDS cases. Some gay men who injected methamphetamines with contaminated needles unknowingly transmitted the HIV virus that causes AIDS. In the late 1990s, meth abuse spread to the rural Midwest and the East Coast, where clinicians and public health officials continued to miss the link between HIV and meth abuse. Clinicians assumed that the white, middle-class, male professionals who attended drug treatment facilities were using cocaine or heroin and did not specifically test for methamphetamine use. Consequently, a new generation of young gay men using methamphetamines may unwittingly trigger another round of AIDS deaths. *AIDS Alert* is a monthly publication that is a source of AIDS news, information, and advice for health care professionals.

Originally manufactured by the Germans in the 1880s and later used by the Japanese to keep military personnel awake on long shifts, methamphetamine first was a significant presence in the Western United States in the late 1940s.

"After the second World War, there were vast stores of

methamphetamine released in the Japanese black market, and methamphetamine use reached epidemic proportions in post-WWII Japan," says E. Michael Gorman, PhD, MPH, MSW, an assistant professor in the College of Social Work at San Jose (CA) State University.

"Supposedly, Americans then were exposed to it and brought it back to the West Coast," Gorman says. For decades, methamphetamine use was limited to the West Coast and Hawaii, becoming popular at various times in a multitude of groups, including Hells Angels, he says. "In the early days, crystal meth was bikers' coffee, literally put into people's coffee and drunk."

Since meth use didn't pose as many law enforcement and social problems as cocaine use, the drug remained under the radar screen and was rarely studied or analyzed, he explains. "But there were a couple of methamphetamine epidemics. One was in the late 1940s and early 1950s, and the other was in the 1970s in San Francisco."

The Latest Meth Epidemic

The latest epidemic began in the late 1990s and has continued into the 21st century, this time spreading across the nation.

Gorman, who has been an AIDS researcher since the beginning of the epidemic, first saw a problem with methamphetamine use in San Francisco's early days of AIDS, before the virus was identified as the culprit behind a rash of strange diseases and deaths.

While working on the first HIV/AIDS studies in San Francisco through the University of California, San Francisco and the San Francisco Health Department, Gorman interviewed gay and bisexual men who were sick with symptoms of AIDS, before the syndrome was named.

These men told Gorman and co-investigators that they had frequented a bathhouse called the Barracks in the late 1970s and early 1980s.

"The Barracks was a methamphetamine emporium," he says. "The drug was prevalent in this institution, which was subsequently shut down, and a lot of people who had histories of this drug were among the earliest AIDS cases."

Researchers were able to document this drug connection to AIDS because of the wide net of questions they asked early AIDS patients. Since the disease's cause was unknown, the virus' first victims were asked questions about every facet of their lives, Gorman says.

However, once researchers discovered that the virus was transmitted sexually and through shared needles of heroin users, the connection with methamphetamine was mostly forgotten, he adds.

"Jump forward to 1993–1994: When working in a treatment clinic, I recognized that these are some of the same crowd I interviewed in the early 1980s," Gorman says. "It was troubling to me, and I saw this HIV connection to methamphetamine and didn't understand how it worked." After interviewing HIV-positive men who had histories of methamphetamine use, including injection drug use with meth, Gorman realized that meth users were a very diverse population, even among homosexuals. "One of the things going on is that this drug for men had a heavy sexual aspect to it. It seemed to be an aphrodisiac," he says.

However, the link between HIV and methamphetamine use largely was ignored until later in the 1990s when meth use spread to the Midwest, rural Western areas, and most recently the East Coast. The availability of methamphetamine on the East Coast is only beginning to be recognized, and it's still not being identified by many clinicians, says Michael C. Clatts, PhD, medical anthropologist and associate professor of public health in the Department of Sociomedical Science at Columbia University in New York City. Clatts also is the director of the Institute for International Research On Youth At Risk at the National Development Research Institutes in New York City.

Drug monitoring systems in New York do not even include

specific questions about methamphetamine, which is grouped with cocaine and other stimulants, Clatts says. "So if someone shows up at a drug treatment center all jazzed up and nervous and fidgety, it's assumed the person's a cocaine user."

Making the Same Mistakes

As a result of public indifference about the growing trend of meth abuse, researchers have witnessed a new wave of drug users among young gay men who are making the same risky behavior mistakes that were made by their counterparts 20 years ago before HIV was identified.

"The new generation of gay men is going to witness the same kind of losses as the older men who saw thousands of their friends and lovers die from AIDS," Clatts says. "The amount of anxiety that exists in the gay community around HIV is very substantial, and that's what in part is fueling some of this methamphetamine use."

If it's been difficult for clinicians and public health officials to recognize methamphetamine use as a problem on the East Coast, the problem is even more invisible in rural and Midwestern communities, where methamphetamine use has become a part of daily life for many.

"The reality is: It's part of the rural economy," Gorman states.

Besides being prevalent in some pockets of the gay and bisexual community, methamphetamine use now has been studied in women, who in some Midwestern states comprise 50% of admissions for metamphetamine treatment.

Working class, Latino, and rural populations have been drawn to the drug for different reasons than the gay population, he says.

"I'm struck by the fact that people do meth for reasons such as they want to work harder, juggle two jobs, and in some cases, to have better sex," Gorman says. "They can do tasks like clean their house, and it's very much an action drug, unlike heroin." Plus, methamphetamine is cheap, giving users a longer and more intense high, and is a favorite drug at youth "rave" parties, he adds.

"It's a poor man's cocaine, and there are parallels with the crack epidemic, which occurred in vulnerable inner-city populations," he says.

Nonetheless, heterosexual men and women who use methamphetamine also are at increased risk for HIV infection, particularly if they inject the drug.

Those who inject methamphetamine may share routes of HIV transmission indirectly, . . . Gorman says.

Keeping Down an HIV Resurgence

Now that methamphetamine use has spread across the United States and to heterosexual populations, it will require concerted private and public health efforts to treat and prevent the problem from causing a resurgence in HIV infection.

He suggests that HIV clinicians begin by asking patients whether they use methamphetamine and whether this use includes injecting the drugs. This is a good start since traditionally prevention programs have focused on asking at-risk individuals about their crack and heroin use, but have ignored methamphetamine, particularly when presented with middle-class, white, professional clients, Gorman says.

"Clinicians fail to understand methamphetamine use," he adds. "If someone is a middle-class male on the West Coast or in a Western U.S. city, the idea that the person also is an injection drug user is mind-boggling, and clinicians wouldn't think to ask."

Baseball Players Pop "Greenies"

Tom Verducci

Baseball players routinely take amphetamines in capsules called "greenies" or "beans" in order to increase their energy and achieve a nervous high. However, the side effects of these illegal drugs include heart problems, stroke, and seizures. Players who use them also can develop addictions to other substances, such as alcohol. Nonetheless, nonusers are sometimes ostracized as slackers and are pressured to take the performance-enhancing pills. Unfortunately, the pills are cheap and readily available in the baseball world. Tom Verducci is a senior writer for *Sports Illustrated*, a weekly sports magazine. He is also coauthor, with Joe Torre, of *Chasing the Dream: My Lifelong Journey to the World Series*.

The idea of playing baseball without taking amphetamines or other stimulants is so absurd to some major leaguers that they have a catchphrase for it: playing naked. There are, of course, varying degrees of nakedness; but the fact remains that popping pills—everything from caffeine tablets to Ritalin to the amphetamine capsules known as greenies or beans—is as standard to many ballplayers' pregame routine as stretching exercises and batting practice.

Amphetamines, particularly, have a long, documented history in baseball. Pete Rose admitted in a 1979 *Playboy* interview that he had used "greenies." Philadelphia Phillies pitcher Randy Lerch testified under oath in 1981 that the physician for

Tom Verducci, "Getting Amped," *Sports Illustrated*, vol. 96, June 3, 2002, p. 23. Copyright © 2002 by Time, Inc. All rights reserved. Reproduced by permission.

the Phillies' Double A Reading affiliate had written him pre-scriptions for amphetamines; several other members of the 1980 world champion Phils were also alleged to have gotten prescriptions for the drugs.

More recently, even more rampant use of stimulants has been confirmed to *Sports Illustrated* by players on a spectrum from heavy users to those who have only observed it. According to 1996 National League MVP [Most Valuable Player] Ken Caminiti, who admits to having taken amphetamines as well as steroids during his 15-year career, there are some teams on which almost everyone uses some kind of stimulant: "You hear it all the time from teammates, 'You're not going to play naked, are you?' Even the guys who are against greenies may be pop-ping 25 caffeine pills, and they're up there [at bat] with their hands shaking. This game is so whacked out that guys will take anything to get an edge. You got a pill that will make me feel better? Let me have it."

Chad Curtis, an outfielder who retired last year [2001] after 10 big league seasons and says he never used performance-enhancing drugs, agrees with Caminiti's approximation that perhaps 90% of the players take some form of pregame stimu-lant. "You might have one team where eight guys play naked and another team where nobody does, but that sounds about right," Curtis says. "Sometimes guys don't even know what they're taking. One guy will take some pills out of his locker and tell somebody else, 'Here, take one of these. You'll feel bet-ter.' The other guy will take it and not even know what it is."

Curtis adds that amphetamine use is so prevalent that nonusers are sometimes ostracized as slackers. "If the starting pitcher knows that you're going out there naked, he's upset that you're not giving him [everything] you can," Curtis says. "The big-time pitcher wants to make sure you're beaning up before the game."

Players today are also using a wider selection of stimulants, both legal and illegal. The choices include over-the-counter medications and supplements such as Ripped Fuel and Ultimate

Orange that contain caffeine or ephedrine—an amphetamine-like stimulant that has been banned by the International Olympic Committee, the NCAA and the NFL—or ephedra, its herbal form. Ephedrine is a central nervous system stimulant that elevates heart rate and blood pressure, making it especially dangerous for people with hypertension.

Dr. John Lombardo, the NFL's adviser on anabolic steroids, warned players and teams . . . that ephedrine has been tied to heart problems, stroke and seizures. The FDA [Federal Drug Administration] recommends that ephedrine not be used for more than one week. Continued usage leads to tolerance of the substance, which may lead to increased dosage, which could produce toxic results.

For a stronger effect, however, players turn to illegally obtained Ritalin, a central nervous system stimulant that is said to sharpen focus and concentration and is often prescribed for children with attention deficit disorder, and greenies—Dexedrine and Adderall are among those commonly prescribed—that are obtained through physicians or drug dealers. "Greenies are easy to get," Caminiti says. "They cost two to three dollars a pill, and guys are buying thousands at a time."

Caminiti, a recovering alcoholic, says he often arrived at the clubhouse lethargic and weary after a night of drinking. Almost immediately after beaning up, Caminiti says, he felt more energetic. "You take some pills, go out and run in the outfield, and you get the blood flowing," he says. "All of a sudden you feel much better. There were other times when you'd say, I feel good enough to play naked today, but you know what? I can feel even better. So you'd take them then, too."

Amphetamines Can Lead to Other Addictions

But Caminiti says now that amphetamines are just as bad as cocaine. "There is a chemical-based dependency that develops. So you're always saying, I feel good, but I can feel better." San Diego Padres general manager Kevin Towers agrees: "Once you get on greenies, it can lead to other addictions, especially alcohol. One brings you up, and one brings you down."

Several players said club trainers do not supply the pills but are fully aware of their extensive use and don't feel obligated to stop it. These days, in fact, it's not uncommon for players to bean up in the clubhouse proper, rather than back rooms and training rooms that are off-limits to the media, and to joke with each other about drug use. [In May 2002] a current All-Star, upon being chided by a former player about sitting out one game, shot back, "That's it. I'm going to take a couple extra beans just for you now," and reached into his locker for some pills.

The Sale of Over-the-Counter Methamphetamine Ingredients Causes Controversy

Joseph Tarnowski

Illegal clandestine meth laboratories have cropped up all over rural America. Lab owners are using ingredients from over-the-counter (OTC) cold medications to illegally produce meth-amphetamines. To combat this practice, new state laws and local ordinances are requiring that grocery store retailers keep these OTC medicines behind the counters and limit their sales. Retailers oppose these measures because they cut into sales, have a negative effect on customer service, and make the store owners liable for those clerks who break the laws. Joseph Tarnowski is a New York–based freelance journalist and former staff member of RetailTech, an online source for retail and food marketing information.

In some rural areas of the United States, over-the-counter [OTC] cough and cold medicines are flying off the shelves, and not because of a flu epidemic. Since the federal Drug Enforcement Administration [DEA] has been cracking down on the diversion and misuse of bulk chemicals to produce metham-

Joseph Tarnowski, "A Cure for the Common Criminal," *Progressive Grocer*, vol. 82, February 1, 2003, p. 65. Copyright © 2003 by VNU Business Media, Inc. Reproduced by permission.

phetamine—commonly known as "speed" or "crank"—illegal drug laboratories have turned to household chemicals and OTC cold remedies for raw materials.

"Methamphetamine is probably the No. 1 drug threat in rural America right now," says DEA public affairs special agent Will Glaspy. "There are multiple ways to manufacture methamphetamine, and there are two key ingredients, ephedrine and pseudoephedrine—and you can get them from OTC cold medicines."

Another meth precursor [ingredient necessary to produce the drug], phenylpropanolamine, has been taken off the market because of its side effects, but leftover supplies may be available in some areas.

What the meth manufacturers are doing, according to Glaspy, is stripping store shelves of these medications and breaking down the time-release capsules to extract the pseudoephedrine. Methamphetamine can be produced by mini-laboratories using relatively common items like mason jars, coffee filters, hot plates, pressure cookers, pillow cases, plastic tubing, and gasoline cans—many of which can easily fit in a suitcase.

The growing use of the Internet, which provides access to methamphetamine recipes, coupled with increased demand for high-purity product, has resulted in an increase in the number of these mini-labs. In 2001, there were more than 7,700 labs with capacities under 10 pounds, according to DEA estimates.

"Theoretically, there is a one-to-one ratio—one gram of pseudoephedrine can make one gram of methamphetamine," says DEA's Glaspy. "In reality, it is more like a 66-percent yield."

A gram of methamphetamine sells for anywhere from $80 to $100 on the street, depending on supply.

Confronting the Issue

Curtis Hartin, director of pharmacy for Schnuck Markets, Inc., has had to confront the situation head-on. "It's not a big problem now, but I can see it mushrooming quickly," he says. The St. Louis–based grocery chain operates pharmacies in 93 of its 101 stores. The meth problem is growing at an increased pace in the Midwest.

To address the situation, DEA administrator Asa Hutchinson visited more than 30 states [in 2002] as part of his "Meth in America: Not in Our Town" tour. Hutchinson stressed the role of community involvement in reducing the nation's rate of methamphetamine production and addiction.

States also have been taking action. Bills are pending in some that would place sales limits on OTC medicines that can be used in the manufacture of methamphetamine. Eight states have already passed laws limiting the sale of these drugs.

Retailers Meth Watch

In North Dakota, Attorney General Wayne Stenejem instituted the Retailers Meth Watch program, a partnership between the attorney general's Bureau of Criminal Investigation and a number of concerned retailers. The program's goals are to raise awareness of the methamphetamine lab problem, to educate and train retail employees to recognize the signs that individuals are obtaining precursors to methamphetamine, and to limit the accessibility of those precursors.

The bureau arranges training sessions for North Dakota retailers and provides a package that contains decals, posters, signage, suspicious transaction reports, and other training aids.

Stenejem is proposing legislation to bar people from buying more than two packages of cold pills at a time.

Colorado has proposed legislation to increase methamphetamine-related penalties. A bill sponsored by Rep. Tim Fritz and Sen. Jim Dyer would make knowingly selling chemicals used to manufacture meth a misdemeanor and impose a fine of $10,000. "Law enforcement has had a record number of meth lab busts in 2002," says Don Hopkins, a spokesman for the governor's office. "All of the ingredients, when purchased separately, are legal, so it is easy to set up clandestine labs. Retail is the best point to stop these producers from gathering the necessary precursors."

"In addition to the state laws, there are local ordinances in the metropolitan St. Louis area that limit specific products that can be sold over the counter," says Schnucks' Hartin. "In some of our stores, all single-source pseudoephedrine has to be behind the counter, under direct supervision of the cashiers. Plus, we set up our cash registers so that no more than three can be sold at once."

Retailers Oppose Mandatory Sales Limits

While retailers agree that there is a problem, many are against mandatory sales limits, which place the burden of compliance on them, particularly on their cashiers. "Many of the fines and penalties against retailers are quite severe, especially when you are trusting a young clerk to be compliant in these issues," says Mary Ann Wagner, v.p. of pharmacy regulatory affairs at the National Association of Chain Drug Stores [NACDS]. "Our position is that we want to work voluntarily to try to address some of these issues."

Customer Inconvenience

In addition to the potential liabilities, some of these laws hinder customer service. "It does create a problem for us," says Hartin. "Our stores are built for self service, so having to move these medicines behind the counter is inconvenient for our customers and limits our access to them. We put up signs at the shelf directing them to the products, but it definitely has had an impact on sales to some degree. Not all of our stores have this problem—it is only a few locations in isolated areas—but all of them in the state are affected."

Retailers are exempt from liability in most cases where they can prove that they acted in good faith to try to comply with the law. "In some cases this may mean positioning security cameras over the cough and cold sections or placing these remedies behind the counter," says Wagner. "But that will not prevent someone from making multiple purchases throughout the day."

And retail sales limits will do nothing to stop those who steal these OTC medicines. Wagner says sales limits may do more harm than good by discouraging business owners from carrying the cough and cold remedies because of the potential liability. In the end, she says, retailers and consumers will be affected, while the meth makers will simply find another way to get their raw materials.

While NACDS opposes mandatory sales limits on meth precursors, Wagner says retailers should exercise vigilance when selling these OTC medicines. "There are a variety of actions that retailers can take, and are making, as good corporate citizens," she says. "The focus should be on training and procedures in selling these medicines, not mandatory sales limits."

Asia's Speed Addiction

Karl Taro Greenfeld

In the early 1990s, methamphetamine use skyrocketed in many Asian countries. After the crash of many of the region's economies later in the decade, abuse of the drug surged again. In this selection, Karl Taro Greenfeld relates his experiences while visiting meth junkies in one of Thailand's major slums. Almost all of the five thousand residents openly sell and use a smokable form of methamphetamine called *yaba* or "mad medicine." The author, who injects the narrative with reflections on his own former methamphetamine use, describes the cycle of drug-induced euphoria followed by an inevitable crashing depression that leaves the user feeling needy and desperate for more of the drug. The addicts Greenfeld describes seem to have lost their hopes of improving their lives. However, the Thai slum drug treatment centers, bleak prisonlike facilities, are overwhelmed by *yaba* abusers seeking help. Sadly, it appears that these people are facing a bleak future. Elsewhere in Asia, methamphetamine production continues to boom as families set up meth labs in bathrooms and farmhouses. Tough drug enforcement laws have had little success in stopping the sale and abuse of methamphetamines. Karl Taro Greenfeld is a journalist and author of *Speed Tribes*.

Jacky talks about killing him, slitting his throat from 3 till 9 and hanging him upside down so the blood drains out of him the way it ran from the baby pigs they used to slaughter in her village before a funeral feast. He deserves it, really, she says, for his freeloading, for his hanging around, for how he just stands there, spindly legged and narrow chested and pimple faced with his big yearning eyes, begging for another hit.

She has run out of methamphetamine, what the Thais call yaba (mad medicine), and she has become irritable and potentially violent. Jacky's cheeks are sunken, her skin pockmarked and her hair an unruly explosion of varying strands of red and brown. She is tall and skinny, and her arms and legs extend out from her narrow torso with its slightly protuberant belly like the appendages of a spider shortchanged on legs.

Sitting on the blue vinyl flooring of her Bangkok hut, Jacky leans her bare back against the plank wall, her dragon tattoos glistening with sweat as she trims her fingernails with a straight razor. It has been two days—no, three—without sleep, sitting in this hut and smoking the little pink speed tablets from sheets of tinfoil stripped from Krong Tip cigarette packets. Now, as the flushes of artificial energy recede and the realization surfaces that there's no more money anywhere in her hut, Jacky is crashing hard, and she hates everyone and everything. Especially Bing. She hates that sponging little punk for all the tablets he smoked a few hours ago—tablets she could be smoking right now. Back then, she had a dozen tablets packed into a plastic soda straw stuffed down her black wireframe bra. The hut was alive with the chatter of half a dozen speed addicts, all pulling apart their Krong Tip packs and sucking in meth smoke through metal pipes. Now that the pills are gone, the fun is gone. And Bing, of course, he's long gone.

This slum doesn't have a name. The 5,000 residents call it Ban Chua Gan, which translates roughly as Do It Yourself Happy Homes. The expanse of jerry-built wood-frame huts with corrugated steel roofs sprawls in a murky bog in Bangkok's Sukhumvit district, in the shadow of 40-story office buildings and glass-plated corporate towers. The inhabitants migrated here about a decade ago from villages all around Thailand. Jacky came from Nakon Nayok, a province near

Bangkok's Don Muang airport, seeking financial redemption in the Asian economic miracle [a time at the end of the twentieth century when Asian economies were flowering]. And for a while in the mid-'90s, conditions in this slum actually improved. Some of the huts had plumbing installed. Even the shabbiest shanties were wired for electricity. The main alleyways were paved. That was when Thailand's development and construction boom required the labor of every able-bodied person. There were shopping malls to be built, housing estates to be constructed, highways to be paved.

Around the same time, mad medicine began making its way into Do It Yourself Happy Homes. It had originally been the drug of choice for long-haul truck and bus drivers, but during the go-go '90s, it evolved into the working man's and woman's preferred intoxicant, gradually becoming more popular among Thailand's underclass than heroin and eventually replacing that opiate as the leading drug produced in the notorious Golden Triangle—the world's most prolific opium-producing region—where Myanmar (Burma), Thailand and Laos come together. While methamphetamines had previously been sold either in powdered or crystalline form, new labs in Burma, northern Thailand and China commoditized the methamphetamine business by pressing little tablets of the substance that now [as of 2001] retail for about 50 baht ($1.20) each. At first only bar girls like Jacky smoked it. Then some of the younger guys who hung out with the girls tried it. Soon a few of the housewives began smoking, and finally some of the dads would take a hit or two when they were out of corn whiskey. Now it has reached the point that on weekend nights, it's hard to find anyone in the slum who isn't smoking the mad medicine.

When the yaba runs out after much of the slum's population has been up for two days bingeing, many of the inhabitants feel a bit like Jacky, cooped up in her squalid little hut, her mouth turned down into a scowl and her eyes squinted and empty and mean. She looks as if she wants something. And if she thinks you have what she wants, look out. She slices at her cuticles with the straight razor. And curses Bing.

But then Bing comes around the corner between two shanties and down the narrow dirt path to Jacky's hut. He stands looking lost and confused, as usual. Jacky pretends he's not there. She sighs, looking at her nails, and stage whispers to me that she hates him.

Bing, his long black hair half-tied into a ponytail, stands next to a cinder-block wall rubbing his eyes. Above his head, a thick trail of red army ants runs between a crack in the wall and a smashed piece of pineapple. He reaches into his pocket and pulls out a tissue in which he has wrapped four doa (bodies, slang for speed tablets). Jacky stops doing her nails, smiles and invites Bing back into her hut, asking sweetly, "Oh, Bing, where have you been?"

This mad medicine is the same drug that's called shabu in Japan and Indonesia, batu in the Philippines and bingdu in China. While it has taken scientists years to figure out the clinical pharmacology and neurological impact of ecstasy and other designer drugs, methamphetamines are blunt pharmaceutical instruments. The drug encourages the brain to flood the synapses with the neurotransmitter dopamine—the substance your body uses to reward itself when you, say, complete a difficult assignment at the office or finish a vigorous workout. And when the brain is awash in dopamine, the whole cardiovascular system goes into sympathetic overdrive, increasing your heart rate, pulse and even your respiration. You become, after that first hit of speed, gloriously, brilliantly, vigorously awake. Your horizon of aspiration expands outward, just as in your mind's eye your capacity for taking effective action to achieve your new, optimistic goals has also grown exponentially. Then, eventually, maybe in an hour, maybe in a day, maybe in a year, you run out of speed. And you crash.

In country after country throughout Asia, meth use skyrocketed during the '90s. And with the crash of the region's high-flying economies, the drug's use has surged again. The base of the drug—ephedrine—was actually first synthesized in

Asia: a team of Japanese scientists derived it from the Chinese mao herb in 1892. Unlike ecstasy, which requires sophisticated chemical and pharmaceutical knowledge to manufacture, or heroin, whose base product, the poppy plant, is a vulnerable crop, ephedrine can be refined fairly easily into meth. This makes meth labs an attractive family business for industrious Asians, who set them up in converted bathrooms, farmhouses or even on the family hearth.

There is something familiar to me about Jacky and her little hut and her desperate yearning for more speed and even for the exhilaration and intoxication she feels when she's on the pipe. Because I've been there. Not in this exact room or with these people. But I've been on speed.

During the early '90s, I went through a period when I was smoking shabu with a group of friends in Tokyo. I inhaled the smoke from smoothed-out tinfoil sheets folded in two, holding a lighter beneath the foil so that the shards of shabu liquefied, turning to a thick, pungent, milky vapor. The smoke tasted like a mixture of turpentine and model glue; to this day I can't smell paint thinner without thinking of smoking speed.

The drug was euphorically powerful, convincing us that we were capable of anything. And in many ways we were. We were all young, promising, on the verge of exciting careers in glamorous fields. There was Trey, an American magazine writer, like me, in his 20s; Hiroko, a Japanese woman in her 30s who worked for a Tokyo women's magazine; Delphine, an aspiring French model; and Miki, an A. and R. [artist-and-repertoire] man for a Japanese record label. When we would sit down together in my Nishi Azabu apartment to smoke the drug, our talk turned to grandiose plans and surefire schemes. I spoke of articles I would write. Delphine talked about landing a job doing a Dior lingerie catalog. Miki raved about a promising noise band he had just signed. Sometimes the dealer, a lanky fellow named Haru, would hang around and smoke with us, and we would be convinced that his future was surely just as bright as all of ours. There was no limit to what we could do, especially if we put our speed-driven minds to work.

It's always that way in the beginning: all promise and potential fun. The drug is like a companion telling you that you're good enough, handsome enough and smart enough, banishing all the little insecurities to your subconscious, liberating you from self doubts yet making you feel totally and completely alive.

I don't know that it helped me write better; I don't believe meth really helps you in any way at all. But in those months, it became arguably the most important activity in my life. Certainly it was the most fun. And I looked forward to Haru's coming over with another $150 baggie of shabu, the drug resembling a little oily lump of glass. Then we would smoke, at first only on weekends. But soon we began to do it on weekdays whenever I had a free evening. At first only with my friends. Then sometimes I smoked alone, Then mostly alone.

The teens and twenty-somethings in Ban Chua Gan also like to smoke yaba, but they look down on Jacky and Bing and their flagrant, raging addictions. Sure, the cool guys in the neighborhood, guys like Big, with a shaved head, gaunt face and sneering upper lip, drop into Jacky's once in a while to score some drugs. Or they'll buy a couple of tablets from Bing's mother, who deals. But they tell you they're different from Bing and the hard-core users. "For one thing," Big alibis, "Bing hasn't left the slum neighborhood in a year. He doesn't work. He doesn't do anything but smoke." (Bing just shrugs when I ask if it's true that he hasn't left in a year. "I'm too skinny to leave," he explains. "Everyone will know I'm doing yaba.") Big has a job as a pump jockey at a Star gas station. And he has a girlfriend, and he has his motorcycle, a Honda GSR 125. This weekend, like most weekends, he'll be racing his bike with the other guys from the neighborhood, down at Bangkok's superslum Klong Toey. That's why tonight, a few days before the race, he is working on his bike, removing a few links of the engine chain to lower the gear ratio and give the bike a little more pop off the line. He kneels down with a lighted candle next to him, his hands greasy and black as he works to reattach the chain to the gear sprockets. Around him a few teenage boys and girls are gathered, smoking cigarettes, some squatting on the balls of their feet, their intent faces peering down at scattered engine pads. The sound is the clatter of adolescent boys. Whether the vehicle in question is a '65 Mustang or a '99 Honda GSR motorcycle, the posturing of the too cool motorhead trying to goose a few more horsepower out of his engine while at the same time look bitchin' in front of a crowd of slightly younger female spectators is identical whether in Bakersfield or Bangkok.

The slang for smoking speed in Thai is keng rot, literally racing, the same words used to describe the weekend motorcycle rallying. The bikers' lives revolve around these two forms of keng rot. They look forward all week to racing their bikes against other gangs from other neighborhoods. And while they profess to have nothing but disgust for the slum's hard-core addicts, by 4 A.M. that night on a mattress laid on the floor next to his beloved Honda, Big and his friends are smoking yaba, and there suddenly seems very little difference between his crowd and Jacky's. "Smoking once in a while, on weekends, that really won't do any harm," Big explains, exhaling a plume of white smoke. "It's just like having a drink," But it's Thursday, I point out. Big shrugs, waving away the illogic of his statement, the drug's powerful reach pulling him away from the need to make sense. He says whatever he wants now, and he resents being questioned. "What do you want from me? I'm just trying to have fun."

In Jacky's hut, Bing and a few bar girls are seated with their legs folded under, taking hits from the sheets of tinfoil. As Jacky applies a thick layer of foundation makeup to her face and dabs on retouching cream and then a coating of powder, she talks about how tonight she has to find a foreign customer so she can get the money to visit her children out in Nakon Nayok. Her two daughters and son live with her uncle. Jacky sees them once a month, and she talks about how she likes to bring them new clothes and cook for them. When she talks about her kids, her almond-shaped eyes widen. "I used to dream of opening a small shop, like a gift shop or a 7-Eleven. Then I could take care of my children and make money. I used to dream about it all the time, and I even believed it was possible, that it was just barely out of reach."

Jacky was a motorbike messenger, shuttling packages back and forth throughout Bangkok's busy Chitlom district until she was laid off after the 1997 devaluation of the baht. "Now I don't think about the gift shop anymore. Smoking yaba pushes thoughts about my children to the back of my mind. It's good for that. Smoking means you don't have to think about the hard times." Bing nods his head, agreeing: "When I smoke, it makes everything seem a little better. I mean, look at this place—how can I stop?"

Bing's mother Yee slips off her sandals as she steps into the hut, clutching her 14-month-old baby. She sits down next to her son, and while the baby scrambles to crawl from her lap, she begins pulling the paper backing from a piece of tinfoil, readying the foil for a smoke. Her hands are a whir of finger-flashing activity—assembling and disassembling a lighter, unclogging the pipe, unwrapping the tablets, straightening the foil, lighting the speed and then taking the hit. She exhales finally, blowing smoke just above her baby's face. Bing asks his mother for a hit. She shakes her head. She doesn't give discounts or freebies, not even to her own son.

I ask Yee if she ever tells Bing he should stop smoking yaba. "I tell him he shouldn't do so much, that it's bad for him. But he doesn't listen."

Perhaps she lacks credibility, since she smokes herself?

"I don't smoke that much," she insists.

"She's right," Bing agrees. "Since she doesn't smoke that much, I should listen to her."

"And he's only 15 years old," Yee adds.

Bing reminds her he's 17.

"I don't know where the years go," Yee says, taking another hit.

For the countries on the front lines of the meth war, trying to address the crisis with tougher enforcement has had virtually no effect on curtailing the numbers of users or addicts. Asia has some of the toughest drug laws in the world. In Thailand, China, Taiwan and Indonesia, even a low-level drug-trafficking or -dealing conviction can mean a death sentence. Yet yaba is openly sold in Thailand's slums and proffered in Jakarta's nightclubs, and China's meth production continues to boom. Even Japan, renowned for its strict antidrug policies, has had little success in stemming speed abuse. Most likely, these countries and societies will have to write off vast swaths of their populations as drug casualties, like the American victims of the '80s crack epidemic.

Asia's medical and psychiatric infrastructure is already being overwhelmed by the number of meth abusers crashing and seeking help. But in most of the region, counseling facilities are scarce, and recovery is viewed as a matter of willpower and discipline rather than a tenuous and slow spiritual and psychological rebuilding process. Drug-treatment centers are usually run like a cross between boot camp and prison. Beds are scarce as addicts seek the meager resources available. In China, for example, the nearly 750 state-run rehab centers are filled to capacity; in Thailand the few recovery centers suffer from a chronic shortage of staff and beds. While the most powerful tools for fighting addiction in the West—12-step programs derived from Alcoholics Anonymous—are available in Asia, they are not widely disseminated and used.

What started out as a diversion for me and my Tokyo crowd degenerated in a few months into the chronic drug use of Jacky and her crowd. I began to smoke alone to begin my days. In the evening I'd take Valium or halcyon or cercine or any of a number of sedatives to help me calm down. When I stopped smoking for a few days just to see if I could, a profound depression would overcome me. Nothing seemed worthwhile. Nothing seemed fun. Every book was torturously slow. Every song was criminally banal. The sparkle and shine had been sucked out of life so completely that my world became a fluorescent-lighted, decolorized, saltpetered version of the planet I had known before. And my own prospects? Absolutely dismal. I would sit in that one-bedroom Nishi Azabu apartment and consider the sorry career I had embarked upon, these losers I associated with compounding the very long odds that I would ever amount to anything.

These feelings, about the world and my life, seemed absolutely real. I could not tell for a moment that this was a neurological reaction brought on by the withdrawal of the methamphetamine. My brain had stopped producing dopamine in normal amounts because it had come to rely upon the speed kicking in and running the show. Researchers now report that as much as 50% of the dopamine-producing cells in the brain can be damaged after prolonged exposure to relatively low levels of methamphetamine. In other words, the depression is a purely chemical state. Yet it feels for all the world like the result of empirical, clinical observation. And then, very logically, you realize there is one surefire solution, the only way to feel better: more speed.

I kept at that cycle for a few years and started taking drugs other than methamphetamine until I hit my own personal bottom. I spent six weeks in a drug-treatment center working out a plan for living that didn't require copious amounts of methamphetamines or tranquilizers. I left rehab five years ago. I haven't had another hit of shabu—or taken any drugs—since then. But I am lucky. Of that crowd who used to gather in my Tokyo apartment, I am the only one who has emerged clean and sober. Trey, my fellow magazine writer, never really tried to quit and now lives back at home with his aging parents. He is nearly 40, still takes speed—or Ritalin or cocaine or whichever uppers he can get his hands on—and hasn't had a job in years. Delphine gave up modeling after a few years and soon was accepting money to escort wealthy businessmen around Tokyo. She finally ended up working as a prostitute. Hiroko did stop taking drugs. But she has been in and out of psychiatric hospitals and currently believes drastic plastic surgery is the solution to her problems. Miki has been arrested in Japan and the U.S. on drug charges and is now out on parole and living in Tokyo. And Haru, the dealer, I hear he's dead.

Despite all I know about the drug, despite what I have seen, I am still tempted. The pull of the drug is tangible and real, almost like a gravitational force compelling me to want to use it again—to feel just once more the rush and excitement and the sense, even if it's illusory, that life does add up, that there is meaning and form to the passing of my days. Part of me still wants it.

At 2 A.M. on a Saturday, Big and his fellow bikers from Do It Yourself Happy Homes are preparing for a night of bike racing by smoking more yaba and, as if to get their 125-cc bikes in a parallel state of high-octane agitation, squirting STP performance goo from little plastic packets into their gas tanks. The bikes are tuned up, and the mufflers are loosened so that the engines revving at full throttle sound like a chain saw cutting bone: splintering, ear-shattering screeches that reverberate up and down the Sukhumvit streets. The bikers ride in a pack, cutting through alleys, running lights, skirting lines of stalled traffic, slipping past one another as they cut through the city smog. This is their night, the night they look forward to all week during mornings at school or dull afternoons pumping gas. And as they ride massed together, you can almost feel the surge of pride oozing out of them, intimidating other drivers to veer out of their way.

On Na Ranong avenue, next to the Klong Toey slum, they meet up with bikers from other slums. They have been holding these rallies for a decade, some of the kids first coming on the backs of their older brothers' bikes. Ken Rot is a ritual by now, as ingrained in Thai culture as the speed they smoke to get up for the night of racing. The street is effectively closed off to non-motorcyclists and pedestrians. The bikers idle along the side of the road and then take off in twos and threes, popping wheelies, the usual motorcycle stunts. But souped up and fitted with performance struts and tires, these bikes accelerate at a terrifying rate, and that blast off the line makes for an unstable and dangerous ride if you're on the back of one of them. It is the internal-combustion equivalent of yaba: fast, fun, treacherous. And likely to result, eventually, in a fatal spill. But if you're young and Thai and loaded on mad medicine, you feel immortal, and it doesn't occur to you that this night of racing will ever, really, have to end.

There are still moments when even hard-core addicts like Jacky can recapture the shiny, bright exuberance of the first few times they tried speed. Tonight, as Jacky dances at Angel's bar with a Belgian who might take her back to his hotel room, she's thinking that she'll soon have enough money to visit her children, and it doesn't seem so bad. Life seems almost manageable. A few more customers, and maybe one will really fall for her and pay to move her to a better neighborhood, to rent a place where even her children could live. Maybe she could open that convenience store after all.

By the next afternoon, however, all the promise of the previous evening has escaped from the neighborhood like so much exhaled smoke. Jacky's customer lost interest and found another girl. Even the bike racing fell apart after the cops broke up the first few rallying points. And now, on a hazy, rainy Sunday, Jacky and a few of the girls are back in her hut. They're smoking, almost desperately uploading as much speed as possible to ward off this drab day and this squalid place.

Jacky pauses as she adjusts the flame on a lighter. "Why don't you smoke?" she asks me.

She tells me it would make her more comfortable if I would join her. I'm standing in the doorway to Jacky's hut. About me are flea-infested dogs and puddles of stagnant water several inches deep with garbage, and all around is the stench of smoldering trash. The horror of this daily existence is tangible. I don't like being in this place, and I find depressing the idea of living in a world that has places like this in it. And I know a hit of the mad medicine is the easiest way to make this all seem bearable. Taking a hit, I know, is a surefire way of feeling good. Right now. And I want it.

But I walk away. And while I hope Jacky and Bing and Big can one day do the same, I doubt they ever can. They have so little to walk toward.

How Drugs Are Classified

The Controlled Substances Act of 1970 classified drugs into five different lists, or schedules, in order of decreasing potential for abuse. The decision to place a drug on a particular schedule is based mainly on the effects the drug has on the body, mind, and behavior. However, other factors are also considered. The schedule is used to help establish the penalties for someone using or selling illegal drugs. On the other hand, sometimes a potentially valuable drug for treating a disease can be incorrectly scheduled, greatly hampering the exploration of its usefulness as a treatment.

Schedule of Controlled Substances

RATING	EXAMPLE
SCHEDULE I A high potential for abuse; no currently accepted medical use in the United States; or no accepted safety for use in treatment under medical supervision.	• Heroin • LSD • Marijuana • Mescaline • MDMA (Ecstasy) • PCP
SCHEDULE II A high potential for abuse; currently accepted medical use with severe restrictions; abuse of the substance may lead to severe psychological or physical dependence.	• Opium and Opiates • Demerol • Codeine • Percodan • Methamphetamines • Cocaine • Amphetamines
SCHEDULE III A potential for abuse less than the substances listed in Schedules I and II; currently accepted medical use in the United States; abuse may lead to moderate or low physical dependence or high psychological dependence.	• Anabolic steroids • Hydrocodone • Certain barbiturates • Hallucinogenic substances

Schedule of Controlled Substances	
RATING	**EXAMPLE**
SCHEDULE IV A low potential for abuse relative to the substances listed in Schedule III; currently accepted medical use in the United States; limited physical or psychological dependence relative to the substances listed in Schedule III.	• Barbiturates • Narcotics • Stimulants
SCHEDULE V A low potential for abuse relative to the substances listed in Schedule III; currently accepted medical use in the United States; limited physical or psychological dependence relative to the substances listed in Schedule IV.	• Compounds with limited codeine such as cough medicine

Facts About Amphetamines

Amphetamines are powerful synthetic stimulant drugs that increase activity in the central nervous system (CNS), leading to increased heart and respiration rates and the dilation of the eyes.

Amphetamines include several specific chemical agents, the most common of which are: amphetamine (Benzedrine), methamphetamine (Desoxyn, Methedrine), dextroamphetamine (Dexedrine), and benzphetamine (Didrex). (Words in parentheses are brand names.)

Amphetamine is structurally related to ephedrine, a natural stimulant found in plants of the genus *Ephedra*. It is also structurally related to adrenaline, the body's "fight or flight" hormone.

Amphetamines can be acquired legally by prescription, but their medical uses are limited. They are used to treat childhood hyperactivity—attention deficit and hyperactivity disorder (ADHD)—and narcolepsy, a rare disorder in which persons are overcome by sudden attacks of deep sleep.

Illicit amphetamines may be sniffed, swallowed, snorted, or injected.

Methamphetamine is the most potent form of amphetamine with or without a prescription. Pharmaceutical methamphetamine was once widely available in the United State, but its medical use is highly restricted today. Almost all methamphetamine is now made in illegal labs.

More than any other illegal drug, methamphetamine is associated with violence and antisocial behavior. It is the most prevalent clandestinely manufactured controlled substance in the United States.

Amphetamine and methamphetamine are usually in powder form in colors ranging from brownish or yellowish to white. The more pure the substance, the more white it will appear.

Crystal methamphetamine is a purified form of the drug. To obtain it, the drug is cleaned, purified, and placed in boiling water, where it is recrystalized into white or clear rocks that are similar to rock candy. Boiling the crystal will turn the substance into a semiliquid called "snot," which can be smoked or placed up the nose.

"Speed" is a term used to describe all the synthetic stimulants, including amphetamine and methamphetamine.

Street names for amphetamine pills and capsules include uppers, white crosses, dexies, bennies, black beauties, sulph, whiz, and phets.

Street names for methamphetamine include crank, meth, crystal, ice, and glass.

"Look-alike" amphetamines are drugs manufactured to look like real amphetamines and mimic their effects. They contain less potent stimulants such as caffeine, ephedrine, and phenylpropanolamine, which are all legal substances. They are expensive and dangerous because the buyer has little way of knowing what they contain.

The effects of amphetamines include the following:
- exhilarating feelings of power and confidence
- energy, focus, and enhanced motivation
- diminished need to sleep or eat
- temporary euphoria followed by intense mental depression and fatigue

The moderate use of amphetamines causes sweating, dilated pupils, increased respiration and pulse, and rapid speech and movement.

Using larger quantities of amphetamines may cause the following:
- dangerously increased heart rate
- paranoia
- hallucinations, including the feeling that bugs are crawling under the skin ("meth bugs")
- aggressiveness
- irritability
- violent behavior (sometimes even murder)
- serious physical deterioration

Chronic use of amphetamines may cause "amphetamine psychosis" (a paranoid delusional state) and long-term brain damage.

1887
German chemist L. Edeleano synthesizes amphetamine, originally named phenylisopropylamine.

1919
Japanese scientist A. Ogata synthesizes methamphetamine.

1927
Amphetamines are used medically as a stimulant and as a nasal decongestant for the first time.

1932
Wholesale drug firm Smith, Kline, and French markets amphetamines as "Benzedrine" in an over-the-counter inhaler to treat congestion.

1935
Physicians use amphetamines to treat narcolepsy (a sleep disorder) and Parkinson's disease.

1937
The American Medical Association approves amphetamines for sale in tablet form for the treatment of narcolepsy and attention deficit hyperactivity disorder (ADHD).

1939–1945
Both amphetamines and methamphetamines are distributed to soldiers in World War II to combat fatigue and heighten endurance.

1950–1953
The U.S. military dispenses amphetamines to troops in the Korean War.

1954
The Japanese amphetamine epidemic reaches its peak, with more than 2 million people using the drug in a population of 88.5 million.

1959
The first intravenous injection of contents from Benzedrine inhalers is reported.

1960
Danish cyclist Kurt Jensen collapses and dies from an amphetamine overdose in the Summer Olympics.

1963
The attorney general of California requests that injectable ampules of amphetamines be removed from the market and illicit speed production begins.

1966–1969
During the Vietnam War, the U.S. Army consumes more amphetamines than the British and American armed forces combined had taken during World War II.

1970
The Comprehensive Drug Abuse Prevention and Control Act is passed in October, and it becomes illegal to possess amphetamines without a prescription.

1971
Amphetamine and methamphetamine (noninjectable) are moved in July from Schedule III to Schedule II of the U.S. Food and Drug Administration listing.

Mid-1970s
MDMA (methylinedioxymethamphetamine) is used by psychiatrists and therapists in the United States.

Early 1980s
MDMA is used nonmedically under the name Ecstasy.

1985
Nonmedical and therapeutic use of MDMA is made illegal.

1996
The U.S. Congress passes the Methamphetamine Control Act, which establishes new controls over key ingredients used to produce the drug, and increases criminal penalties for possession, distribution, and manufacturing of the drug.

2002
Over nine thousand clandestine methamphetamine labs reportedly are seized in the United States.

The editors have compiled the following list of organizations concerned with the issues debated in this book. The descriptions are derived from materials provided by the organizations. All have publications or information available for interested readers. The list was compiled on the date of publication of the present volume; the information provided here may change. Be aware that many organizations take several weeks or longer to respond to inquiries, so allow as much time as possible.

American Council for Drug Education (ACDE)
164 W. 74th St., New York, NY 10023
(800) 488-DRUG (3784) • fax: (212) 595-2553
Phoenix House (212) 595-5810, ext. 7860
e-mail: acde@phoenix.org • Web site: www.acde.org

ACDE informs the public about the harmful effects of abusing drugs and alcohol. It gives the public access to scientifically based, compelling prevention programs and materials. ACDE has resources for parents, youth, educators, prevention professionals, employers, health care professionals, and other concerned community members who are working to help America's youth avoid the dangers of drug and alcohol abuse.

Centers for the Application of Prevention Technologies (CAPT)
Central regional contact: Minnesota Institute of Public Health
2720 Highway 10, Mounds View, MN 55112
(800) 782-1878 • fax: (763) 427-7841
Web site: www.captus.org

CAPT seeks to bring research into practice by assisting states and community-based organizations in applying the latest research-based information to their substance abuse prevention programs, practices, and policies. CAPT provides information for substance abuse prevention as well as top stories on drug research and legislation. It offers a science-based prevention primer.

Drug Enforcement Administration (DEA)
2401 Jefferson Davis Highway, Alexandria, VA 22301
(202) 307-1000
Web site: www.usdoj.gov/dea

The DEA is the federal agency charged with enforcing the nation's drug laws. The agency concentrates on stopping the smuggling and distribution of narcotics in the United States and abroad. It has information on drugs and drug trafficking as well as recent cases and major operations. It offers state fact sheets, news releases, speeches, and testimony, and publishes the *Drug Enforcement Magazine* three times a year.

Lindesmith Center
70 W. 36th St., 16th Fl., New York, NY 10018
(212) 613-8020 • fax: (212) 613-8021
Web site: www.lindesmith.org

The Lindesmith Center is a policy research institute that focuses on broadening the debate on drug policy and related issues. The center houses a library and information center; organizes seminars and conferences; acts as a link between scholars, government, and the media; directs a grant program in Europe; and undertakes projects on topics such as methadone policy reform and alternatives to drug testing in the workplace. The center publishes fact sheets on topics such as needle and syringe availability, drug prohibition, the U.S. prison system, and drug education.

Narcotic Educational Foundation of America (NEFA)
28245 Crocker Ave., Suite 230, Santa Clarita, CA 91355-1201
(661) 775-6960 • fax: (661) 775-1648
e-mail: info@cnoa.org • Web site: www.cnoa.org/NEFA.htm

NEFA was founded in 1924 to educate the public about the dangers of drug abuse. NEFA conducts research and has produced printed materials on aspects of drug abuse. A referral service and a speakers bureau are available. NEFA publishes pamphlets on such subjects as glue sniffing, cocaine, alcohol, amphetamines, heroin, and drug addiction, emphasizing the effects and dangers of drugs. A series of student reference sheets on drugs is distributed, including: *Barbiturates, Anabolic Steroids, Drug Dependence, Drugs and the Automotive Age, Inhalants, PCP, Prescription Drugs, Marijuana,* and *Tobacco.*

National Center on Addiction and Substance Abuse at Columbia University (CASA)
633 Third Ave., 19th Fl., New York, NY 10017
(212) 841-5200 • fax: (212) 956-8020
Web site: www.casacolumbia.org

CASA is a private, nonprofit organization that works to educate the public about the costs and hazards of substance abuse and the prevention and treatment of all forms of chemical dependency. The center supports treatment as the best way to reduce drug addiction. It produces publications describing the harmful effects of alcohol and drug addiction and effective ways to address the problem of substance abuse. It publishes an annual report and newsletter.

National Institute on Drug Abuse (NIDA)
U.S. Department of Health and Human Services
6001 Executive Blvd., Rm. 5213 MSC 9561, Bethesda, MD 20892-9561
(301) 443-1124
e-mail: Information@lists.nida.nih.gov • Web site:
www.nida.nih.gov

NIDA supports and conducts research on drug abuse—including the yearly Monitoring the Future Survey—to improve addiction prevention, treatment, and policy efforts. It publishes the bimonthly *NIDA Notes* newsletter, the periodic *NIDA Capsules* fact sheets, and a catalog of research reports and public education materials covering such topics as the nature and extent of drug abuse.

Office of National Drug Control Policy (ONDCP)

Executive Office of the President, Drugs and Crime Clearinghouse
PO Box 6000, Rockville, MD 20849-6000
(800) 666-3332 • fax: (301) 519-5212
e-mail: ondcp@ncjrs.org • Web site:
www.whitehousedrugpolicy.gov

ONDCP is responsible for formulating the government's national drug strategy and the president's antidrug policy as well as coordinating the federal agencies responsible for stopping drug trafficking. It provides fact sheets and information on drugs. Drug policy studies are available upon request.

Partnership for a Drug-Free America

405 Lexington Ave., Suite 1601, New York, NY 10174
(212) 922-1560 • fax: (212) 922-1570
Web site: www.drugfreeamerica.org

The Partnership for a Drug-Free America is a nonprofit organization that utilizes media communication to reduce demand for illicit drugs in America. Best known for its national antidrug advertising campaign, the partnership works to "unsell" drugs to children and to prevent drug use among kids. It publishes the annual *Partnership Newsletter* as well as monthly press releases about current events with which the partnership is involved.

RAND Distribution Services

1700 Main St., PO Box 2138, Santa Monica, CA 90407-2138
(310) 393-0411 • fax: (310) 451-6996
Web site: www.rand.org

The RAND Corporation is a research institution that seeks to improve public policy through research and analysis. RAND's Drug Policy Research Center publishes information on the costs, prevention, and treatment of alcohol and drug abuse as well as on trends in drug-law enforcement. Its extensive list of publications includes a report on the project Methamphetamine Abuse—Natural History, Treatment Effects by Mary-Lynn Brecht.

FOR FURTHER RESEARCH

Books

Rob Alcraft, *Need to Know: Amphetamines*. Port Melbourne, Australia: Heinemann Education Books, 2000.

John Ashcroft, *Midwest Methamphetamine Crisis: Developing a Plan for Federal, State, and Local Cooperation*. Collingdale, PA: DIANE, 1999.

Linda N. Bayer, *Amphetamines and Other Uppers*. New York: Chelsea House, 1999.

Peter Breggin, *Reclaiming Our Children*. Cambridge, MA: Perseus Books, 2000.

——, *Talking Back to Ritalin*. Monroe, MA: Common Courage, 1998.

William S. Burroughs, *Speed*. New York: Overlook, 1984.

Julian Chomer, *Speed and Amphetamines*. New York: Franklin Watts, 1990.

Lawrence Clayton and Ruth C. Rosen, *Amphetamines and Other Stimulants*. New York: Rosen, 1994.

Allan B. Cobb, *Speed and Your Brain: The Incredibly Disgusting Story*. New York: Rosen, 2000.

Sean Connolly, *Amphetamines (Just the Facts)*. Port Melbourne, Australia: Heinemann Library, 2000.

J. Frederick Garman, *Methamphetamine and "Ice."* Elizabethtown, PA: William Gladden Foundation, 1992.

Brent Q. Hafen and David Soulier, *Amphetamines: Facts, Figures, and Information*. Ontario, Canada: Hazelden Information Education, 1990.

Hillary Klee, *Amphetamine Misuse: International Perspectives on Current Trends*. London: Dunitz Martin, 1997.

John Knoerle, *Crystal Meth Cowboys*. Chicago: Blue Steel, 2003.

David Lenson, *On Drugs*. Minneapolis: University of Minnesota Press, 1995.

Richard Lingeman, *Drugs from A to Z: A Dictionary*. New York: McGraw-Hill, 1969.

Mary Ann Littell, *Speed and Methamphetamine Drug Dangers.* Berkeley Heights, NJ: Enslow, 1999.

Scott E. Lukas, *Amphetamines: Danger in the Fast Lane.* New York: Chelsea House, 1985.

Leslie E. Moser, *Crack, Cocaine, Methamphetamine, and Ice.* El Paso: Multi-Media Production, 1990.

Cardwell C. Nuckols, *The Ice Storm: Methamphetamine Revisited.* Ontario, Canada: Hazelden Information Education, 1990.

Michael Pellowski, *Amphetamine Drug Dangers.* Berkeley Heights, NJ: Enslow, 2001.

Jay Schleifer, *Methamphetamines: Speed Kills.* New York: Rosen, 1999.

David E. Smith, *Uppers and Downers.* Upper Saddle, NJ: Prentice-Hall, 1973.

Elizabeth Wurtzel, *More, Now, Again: A Memoir of Addiction.* New York: Simon and Schuster, 2001.

Errol Yudko, *Methamphetamine Use: Clinical and Forensic Aspects.* London: CRC, 2003.

Periodicals

Khabir Ahmad, "Asia Grapples with Spreading Amphetamine Abuse," *Lancet,* May 31, 2003.

L. Aiken, "All About 'Ice,'" *Good Housekeeping,* February 1990.

Jack Anderson, "GI Drug Abuse Hushed Up," *Washington Post,* August 4, 1970.

Felix Belair Jr., "House Cites Rise in GI Drug Use," *New York Times,* May 25, 1971.

James Bovard, "Unsafe at Any Speed," *American Spectator,* April 1996.

Eric G. Boyce, "Use and Effectiveness of Performance-Enhancing Substances," *Journal of Pharmacy Practice,* January 2003.

Anne Marie Brooks, "Danger on Ice," *Current Health 2,* December 1992.

Jordi Cami and Magi Farre, "Drug Addiction," *New England Journal of Medicine,* September 4, 2003.

Marjorie Centofanti, "When Speed Slows You Down," *Psychology Today,* January/February 1997.

Patricia Chisholm, "The ADD Dilemma," *Maclean's*, March 11, 1996.

Arthur K. Cho, "Ice: A New Dosage Form of an Old Drug," *Science*, August 10, 1990.

Per Ola D'Aulaire and Emily D'Aulaire, "A Dangerous Drug Hits the Heartland," *Reader's Digest*, April 1999.

Robert Draper, "Drugs in Small-Town America and Women's Lives in Chaos," *Glamour*, January 1997.

Rich Fee, "Lock Out Meth Makers," *Successful Farming*, August 1999.

Michael R. Fitzgerald, "A Demon Stalks the Land," *Reader's Digest*, February 1994.

Mike Freeman and Buster Olney, "New Drug Tests in Baseball Stir Debate Among Players," *New York Times*, April 22, 2003.

Nancy P. Gibbs, "The Age of Ritalin," *Time*, November 30, 1998.

J.M. Graham, "Amphetamine Politics on Capitol Hill: Passage of Comprehensive Drug Abuse Prevention Act of 1970," *Trans-Action*, January 1972.

Health and Medicine Weekly, "Amphetamine Use Increases in U.S. Workforce," June 23, 2003.

Joshua A. Israel and Kewchang Lee, "Amphetamine Usage and Genital Self-Mutilation," *Addiction*, September 2002.

Marilyn Kalfus, "Speed Is the Drug of Choice Among Pregnant Women," Knight-Ridder/Tribune News Service, August 28, 1996.

Janette M. Kenny, "Danger: Death Lives Here," *Listen*, March 2001.

Kurt Kleiner, "Drug Use Dulls Brain's Response to Novelty," *New Scientist*, August 30, 2003.

John C. Kramer, Vitezslav Fischman, Don C. Littlefield, "Amphetamine Abuse Pattern and Effects of High Doses Taken Internally," *Journal of the American Medical Association*, July 31, 1967.

Daniel A. Labianca, "The Drug Scene's New 'Ice' Age," *USA Today*, January 1992.

Richard Lacayo, "How Sick Was J.F.K.?" *Time*, December 2, 2002.

Anthony R. Lovett, "Wired in California," *Rolling Stone*, May 5, 1994.

Dan McGraw, "The Iowan Connection," *U.S. News & World Report*, March 2, 1998.

Greg Miller, "Speed May Slow Learning," *Science Now*, August 26, 2003.

Judy Monroe, "Ice Shatters Lives," *Current Health 2*, October 1997.

John B. Murray, "Psychophysiological Aspects of Amphetamine-Methamphetamine Abuse," *Journal of Psychology*, March 1998.

Shari Roan, "Can These Pills Kill?" *American Health*, October 1996.

L.S. Robinson, "Raising Stakes in U.S. Mexican Drug Wars," *U.S. News & World Report*, October 5, 1998.

Alex Ross, "The New Suburban High," *Good Housekeeping*, September 1995.

E. Rover, "Rethinking Diet Pills," *Ladies' Home Journal*, March 1997.

Mike Sager, "The Ice Age," *Rolling Stone*, February 8, 1990.

Saturday Evening Post, "Treating Obesity," September/October 1992.

Duncan M. Stanton, "Drug Use in Vietnam: A Survey Among Army Personnel in the Two Northern Corps," *Archives of General Psychiatry*, March 26, 1972.

Anne Mari Sund and Pal Zeiner, "Does Extended Medication with Amphetamine or Methylphenidate Reduce Growth in Hyperactive Children?" *Nord Journal of Psychiatry*, no. 1, 2002.

Time, "There Is No Safe Speed," January 8, 1996.

William K. Urgant Jr., "Addiction in Vietnam: Coming Home with a Habit," *Nation*, July 5, 1971.

Gordon Witkin, "A New Drug Gallops Through the West," *U.S. News & World Report*, November 13, 1995.

Web Sites

Amphetamines.com, www.amphetamines.com. This Web site provides information on the history of amphetamine use and describes the effects of using methamphetamines.

Erowid, www.erowid.org/chemicals/amphetamines/amphetamines.shtml. This site provides general information about amphetamines as well as the history of the drug. It includes research, journal articles, and personal accounts by people who have taken amphetamines.

The Good Drugs Guide, www.thegooddrugsguide.com/amphetamines/ index.htm. This Web site offers basic information about amphetamines, including their effects and the treatment of amphetamine addiction. It includes frequently asked questions and related links.

Indiana Prevention Resource Center, www.drugs.indiana.edu/druginfo/ stimulants.html. The site provides information on stimulants, including fact sheets and documents about amphetamines. It provides governmental and other Web sites that have information on stimulants.

Minnesota Department of Health, www.health.state.mn.us/divs/eh/ meth/sidelinks.html. This Web site offers information about methamphetamine labs, including descriptions of chemicals used to make the drugs, and the dangers of methamphetamine production. It also offers a response manual for those interested in what to do if they find a meth lab.

INDEX

Piness, George, 21
Pool, Robert, 14, 50
Preminger, Otto, 44
Presley, Elvis, 45
Priority Targeting Program, 107
pseudoepinephrine, 84–85
 seizures of, 104
psychosis, 25–26
 in Japan, 33, 34

raves, 127–28
Rawlin, John William, 37
Retailers Meth Watch program,
 141
Ritalin, 137
Rose, Pete, 135

Saiki, Patricia, 75
El-Samad, Norma, 108
San Francisco Amphetamine
 Research Project, 57
Sapienza, Frank, 69
Schmidt, C.F., 21
Schuster, Charles, 71
Seiden, Lewis, 71
Shaw, Mark, 44
Siegel, Ronald, 71
Sills, Jack, 94
Smith, Lynn M., 121
Smith, Roger C., 57, 59, 60, 63,
 65
Solotaroff, Paul, 111
South Korea, as source of black
 market methamphetamines,
 75–76

"speed factories," 60
speed freaks, 56–65
"splash," 37–42
Stalcup, Alex, 116
State Palace Theatre
 investigation, 128
Stenejem, Wayne, 141
Stump, Jane, 77
sympathomimetic amines, 20

Tarnowski, Joseph, 139
Thailand, epidemic in, 144–47,
 149–52, 154–56
Time (magazine), 22, 43
Towers, Kevin, 137–38

users, profile of, 62–64

Verducci, Tom, 135

Wagner, Mary Ann, 142, 143
Weaver, Randy, 83
weight loss, 50
Williams, Tennessee, 44
Wilson, Ed, 80
withdrawal, 54–55, 64
Witkin, Gordon, 79
women, use by, 133
 during pregnancy, 92–97
World War II, 13–14, 26–27
Wright, Tammy, 92, 97
Wyden, Ron, 81

Yamaguchi, Tad, 73–74